The
Busy Woman's
Guide to a
Balanced Life

The
Busy Woman's
Guide to a
Balanced Life

from *Today's Christian Woman* magazine

RAMONA CRAMER TUCKER

Tyndale House Publishers, Inc.
Wheaton, Illinois

Table of Contents

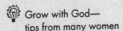

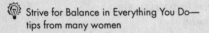

Acknowledgments

Today's Christian Woman magazine and Tyndale House Publishers would like to thank the following people, who graciously gave their permission to use the following material from *Today's Christian Woman* in this book.

ALDRICH, SANDRA P. "Do You Have In-Laws or Out-Laws?" (November/December 1996). Adapted from *Men Read Newspapers, Not Minds,* © 1996 by Sandra P. Aldrich. Used by permission of Tyndale House Publishers, Inc. All rights reserved.

BAILEY, SUSAN M. "In the Red" (November/December 1992).

BARTON, R. RUTH. "Be Content with What You Have" (May/June 1997).

BENCE, KATHY. "Making Guests Feel at Ease" and "Mother's Little Helpers" (November/December 1987).

BRESTIN, DEE. "Hang On to Your Friends" (March/April 1990).

BUDZOWSKI, BONNIE. "Marriage Prayers for Busy Days" (January/February 1991).

COKER, SUSAN. "What's to Celebrate About Being Single?" (November/December 1995).

COUCHMAN, JUDITH. "Alone Doesn't Mean Lonely" (July/August 1990).

MILLER, HOLLY G. "7 Ways to Respond to Failure" (January/February 1994); "Walk Your Way to Fitness" (May/June 1995).

MITTELSTAEDT, ELIZABETH. "Living by God's Promises" (January/February 1995).

NEWENHUYSE, ELIZABETH CODY. "Spring, Summer, Fall Housecleaning" (September/October 1992); "Cultivating Contentment" (September/October 1995).

PATTERSON, LAURETTA. "No Time to Entertain" (January/February 1991).

PETROSKY, DEBRA. "Curb Compulsive Spending" (November/December 1990).

REISSER, DR. PAUL. "Making the Most of Your Doctor Visit" (September/October 1995).

ROBERTS, FAYE L. "The Runaway" (July/August 1993).

ROLLINS, CATHERINE E. "10 Things You Can Say to Make Someone's Day" (May/June 1992).

SHAFTER, RENATE. "I Couldn't Love My Body" (May/June 1996).

SILVIOUS, JAN. "'Tis the Time of Sibling Stress" (November/December 1990).

SMITH, KAY DeKALB. "Bartering Is Back" (January/February 1993).

SNEED, DRS. SHARON AND DAVID. "Why Am I Always So Tired?" (September/October 1990); "Nutrition on the Go" (November/December 1991).

STRUCK, JANE JOHNSON. "Entertaining with Style" (November/December 1987).

TURNER, DENISE. "Old-Fashioned Advice for Today" (November/December 1987).

VAN REKEN, RUTH E. "If You Think You're 'Nothing Special' . . . Think Again" (January/February 1996).

WHELCHEL, MARY. "Reduce Workplace Stress" (November/December 1991); "Should I Downscale My Career?" (January/February 1992); "I Can't Get Any Work Done at Home" (May/June 1993).

WILKINS, LEIGH. "Tuning In to the Holy Spirit" (November/December 1994).

WRIGHT, VINITA HAMPTON. "Can Singles and Marrieds Still Be Friends?" (March/April 1995); "Time for a Little TLC" (May/June 1995).

YATES, SUSAN ALEXANDER. "Nag, Nag, Nag" (July/August 1995); "Is Your Family's Schedule Driving You Crazy?" (September/October 1995).

Introduction: Balancing Act

HAVE YOU EVER

- wished you could get off the busy roller coaster of life, even for a day?
- thought about your home "to do" list at work and your work "to do" list at home?
- longed for friends who would encourage you instead of drain you?
- wished you felt better about yourself or your marriage?
- dreamed of the day you wouldn't have to worry about money?
- hoped your child would take a longer nap just to give you time to think?
- wanted to be in better shape physically— and spiritually?

If so, you aren't the only one. Research done over the past twenty years by *Today's Christian Woman* magazine shows that all women long for more balanced lives. They want to be better parents or to be more comfortable with their single life. They long for financial security, for friends they can count on (and they want to be that kind of friend, too). They want to be in shape physically, for their health's sake.

They want to be hospitable but learn how and when to say no without feeling guilty. They dream about happy, growing marriages and meaningful work. And, most of all, they long to grow closer to God.

If you're longing for balance in your life, then *The Busy Woman's Guide to a Balanced Life* is uniquely suited to you. It gives guidance and practical encouragement for the "Top Ten" areas of a woman's life:

- Family and Parenting
- Finances
- Friendship
- Health and Fitness
- Home and Hospitality
- Marriage
- Self
- Single Life
- Spiritual Life
- Work

Each chapter includes quotes from well-known people like Rachael Crabb, CeCe Winans, and Larry Burkett; ideas from experts on that particular topic; steps, quick tips, and even humorous strategies from a variety of women for balancing your life; and a "Think It Over" section to help you evaluate how you're doing, decide where you'd like to be, then assist you in putting your plan into action.

As busy women, we will always perform a "balancing act" between our roles at home, at work, and in the church and community. According to *Webster's Dictionary,* a balancing act is "the attempt to cope with several often conflicting factors or situations at the same time." When I read that in my own search for balance, I laughed (it was better than crying) because it was and still is a perfect definition of my life as a woman.

But how do we go about this balancing act? That's what *The Busy Woman's Guide to a Balanced Life* is all about. And as we plunge in together, let's remember this: God is our balance, our hope, and our guide. He knows us intimately, and he wants us to give all areas of our life to him. When we turn to him for help and wisdom, he often gives us far more than we ask for. I believe, with all my heart, what the classic author Oswald Chambers once said: "We live by God's surprises." So get ready to discover the surprises God has in store for you as you strive to lead a more balanced life!

Ramona Cramer Tucker

Family and Parenting

Arkansas is where my two best girlfriends—
my sisters—live. For a long time they were just
my messy baby sisters, eight and twelve years
younger. I loved them, but they weren't really
"friends." As they got older, though, an amazing
transformation took place—
they were the ones I called to have lunch with,
to go antiquing with, or to explore country roads
with in my truck. Even when we don't see each other
for a while, we pick up where we left off because we
have a closeness that only comes from
knowing someone intimately.

TWILA PARIS

HOW'S YOUR FAMILY FARING?

THE sister who borrowed your sweater—and returned it a year later. The brother who teased you mercilessly at home but decked the school bully for you. The mom who potty trained you, hugged you when your first date stood you up, and cried when you went to college. The dad who proudly passed bubble-gum cigars at your birth, gave you your first spanking, and bought your first car. The man you fell in love with and married—only to find his parents and siblings were part of the package.

What do these people have in common? They're all part of your wonderful (and frustrating) family. This chapter offers guidance—and humor—for your complex family relationships. And when all else fails, before you speak your mind, remember what speaker/author Anne Ortlund says: "Your family—whatever the combination of humans under your roof—is a mystery, a marvel, a wonder. God has put you together, and God is powerfully at work!"

ARE YOU INVOLVED IN SO MANY CAR POOLS THAT YOU can't remember whether you're coming or going? Do you wonder if you'll *ever* have a family meal again, now that your kids are teenagers? If your family's schedule is driving you crazy, maybe it's time to take control of your schedule—and take your life back. Try these suggestions from family expert Susan Alexander Yates to help you be a better, and more relaxed, parent.

Get Your Schedule under Control

SUSAN ALEXANDER YATES

As I was sitting with several other mothers at a soccer game my daughters were playing in, we began to talk about our kids. One mom described a new dance program her daughter was joining. Another mom began talking about another soccer league in which her child also played. I listened as each mom described all the other clubs her child was involved in.

My children aren't doing everything these girls are, I thought, feelings of guilt and inadequacy rising up in me. *Am I damaging my daughters because they aren't taking advantage of all these activities? Should they join more activities? Am I a good mother?*

But the thought of adding activities to our already-crowded schedule was overwhelming. I knew it would only lead to one more evening of eating in shifts, carpooling kids, and not really connecting with each other.

I was in danger of succumbing to adult peer pressure—a pressure that subtly says, *My child does more than yours does.*

It's easy to become swamped with things to do in a culture with too many good options—and find ourselves feeling like slaves to activity. How can we get our schedule under control?

FIRST THINGS FIRST

The good news is, God doesn't expect us to live in such a complex world without giving us guidelines. He has given us his two great commandments to enable us to make wise decisions.

Jesus said that the greatest commandments are "Love the Lord your God with all your heart and with all your soul and with all your mind" and "Love your neighbor as yourself" (Matt. 22:37, 39).

If I could pinpoint one thing that could help families, it's taking time to sit down together at dinner.

MARILYN QUAYLE

Because my first commitment is to love the Lord, I know my top priority needs to be a daily time with my heavenly Father. Setting aside time to read the Bible and pray enables me to know God better and to understand his love and desires for my life. He cares about a difficult child, an elderly family member, a sticky relationship with a co-worker. He wants to hear what's on my mind, forgive my sins, give me hope, and help me make wise decisions about my family's schedule.

Often I begin each morning by reading a psalm and a proverb. I pray for each family member and our schedules for that day. Spending time alone with God restores my perspective.

DON'T IGNORE YOUR MARRIAGE

The second commandment is "Love your neighbor as yourself." If we're married, our closest neighbor is our spouse. But since ours is a child-oriented society, it's tempting to focus on the kids and put our marriage on hold, assuming we'll spend time together "when things calm down."

The truth is, things don't calm down. Life just gets more

complicated. We need to take time *now* to cultivate our marriage.

Before John and I married, a wise couple challenged us to go out on a date one night a week. We started this habit twenty-six years ago, and although we haven't made it every week, we've made it 65 percent of the time. It hasn't always been easy. When our five kids were young, we often had to get two baby-sitters to handle the crowd! I remember one night before we went out, I fed the children while our daughter Allison said the blessing. "Dear God," she prayed, "please help the baby-sitters to be able to handle us." That was a genuine need in our family!

For several years John and I went out to breakfast one morning a week. Now we do Tuesday lunches. This weekly date has made a big difference in our marriage and given us time to communicate despite busy schedules.

BUILD FAMILY UNITY

Not only do we need time to nurture our marriage, we need to build into our schedules time to encourage relationships between all family members.

Family meals can be a real celebration, but eating together sometimes means saying no to another sport for your child or that church committee you wanted to serve on. When faced with these decisions, ask yourself, Ten years from now, will the choice I make today have been the best one to help my family members grow in love for one another?

When our kids were young, we designated one night each week as "family" night. The youngest kids colored placemats and decorated napkins. Sometimes we asked our kids such questions as, "What would you do if you were president for a day?" or "What would you do if you were given one million dollars?" Occasionally we acted out Bible stories, and often we lined up tall cleaning containers on the kitchen floor and bowled with tennis balls.

It's also important to build traditions with your children.

When our oldest son, John Jr., was in high school, my husband took him out to breakfast early before school one morning a week. Frequently they read the Bible together, often they prayed, and sometimes they simply talked about what was going on in each of their lives. It became a special father-son tradition. So when our second son, Chris, reached tenth grade, he joined his dad and brother. These times have created strong bonds between my three men—bonds that continue even though our boys are now in college.

Family life would be a lot more joyful if parents weren't so uptight. We worry too much. We forget that God's parenting our children, too. We can guide them, but in the end it's up to them and God to write the final chapter of their lives.

VALERIE BELL

LEARN THE ACT OF POSTPONEMENT
There's no way family members can "do it all," so take time to assess your family's needs and set some reasonable goals. Write in couple dates and family times on your calendars. As you determine your schedule, think about the following questions:

- When will I spend time alone with God each day?
- When will we have regular dates to nurture our marriage relationship?
- When will we be together as a family? What meals will we commit to eating together? What time will they be?
- Are there other special times to be with each child?
- Is there flexibility in my schedule for the unexpected?
- What good things will we have to say no to in order for our relationships to develop?

Each family is different—but when we keep God's great commandments in mind, we have a guideline for making wise choices. When we learn to say no to more activities and yes to nurturing family relationships, the results are invaluable.

HOW DO YOU HANDLE YOUR SIBLINGS?

- "I pray, talk with a friend, and sometimes cry."
- "I take a deep breath and ask God to help me forgive."
- "I block her out."
- "I get angry."

If these—or others—are your response to your sister or brother, you're not alone. Sometimes siblings are a royal pain. But because God has called us to love others, *including our siblings*, we need to do our best to improve our relationship with them. How do we go about it? Read on for some great ideas.

Do Your Best to Improve Adult Sibling Relationships

JAN SILVIOUS

If you are dissatisfied with the status quo of your adult sibling relationships, don't give up. There *is* hope. Here are some steps you can take to improve your sibling connections.

1. If you really desire a change, examine yourself first. Are you domineering, condescending, or critical? Do you view your sibling as a "pain"? Until you confess your wrong attitude to God and to your sibling, you will be shut out and resented. So be willing to humble yourself, acknowledge your own wrong behavior, and accept your responsibility to change.

2. Prepare yourself to be with your siblings. Decide what your response will be when you know you'll be around that irritating sibling. If you really want a right relationship with your sibling, remember the scriptural admonition to "be quick to listen, slow to speak and slow to become angry, for man's anger does not bring about the righteous life that God desires" (James 1:19-20).

3. Take your brother or sister seriously. "I still tend to treat my younger brother like the goofy, irresponsible kid he used to be," says Linda. "But in reality he's married, has kids, and is doing well in his career." Give your sibling the respect that adults give one another—even if your sibling refuses to acknowledge *your* adulthood. If you are adamant about change, it must begin with you, no matter how anyone else responds.

4. Express a genuine interest in your brother's or sister's family. Make an effort to talk with your in-laws (yes, even the difficult ones) and your nieces and nephews about their lives. Your encouragement could go miles toward opening the door to a sibling's heart.

5. Communicate with one another. Many families are either bound by silence or energized by arguments. Neither qualifies as true communication. Take time to listen as well as to express your own view. If you need to hammer out a long-standing conflict, find a private time and place.

6. Remember that you're in control. If needed, limit the time you spend with your brother or sister. Also, pray for your sibling—a powerful investment in his or her life—and "clothe yourselves with compassion, kindness, humility, gentleness and patience. Bear with each other and forgive whatever grievances you may have against one another. Forgive as the Lord forgave you" (Col. 3:12-13).

Changes in your sibling connections require changes in your life. If you view the process as an adventure in discovering God's best, you won't be defeated by setbacks and rejections. Once you have committed yourself to a plan for change that honors God and gives respect to your sibling—as well as to yourself—you will discover new strength and deeper insights in your journey toward maturity.

WHEN'S THE LAST TIME SOMEONE DID SOMETHING SPECIAL for you? For me it was two weeks ago. Knowing I was feeling overwhelmed with housework and deadlines, a friend arrived with a steaming casserole in hand—and a mop to scrub my kitchen floor. I felt like a princess because I knew *someone cared*.

Because we live day in and day out with our families, it's easy to forget that they, like our friends, need to feel special. Following are some ideas to get you started. How about trying one out this week on an unsuspecting family member?

TREAT EACH OTHER AS SPECIAL

💡 SPECIAL GUEST Plan a "Guest of Honor" dinner for someone who's under a lot of pressure. Dress up, get out your best china, and eat by candlelight.
KATHY PEEL

💡 PRAYER DOES CHANGE THINGS Your greatest responsibility as a parent is to pray for your children. When we pray, we're reminded that God created them—and loves them even more than we do.
SUSAN ALEXANDER YATES

💡 MISSING PERSON BULLETIN When a family member can't be with you to celebrate an occasion, have everyone present hold up a big sign that says "We miss you!" Take a picture and mail it to the missing person.
JUDIE BYRD

💡 A WARM FUZZY A DAY Affirm each family member. Your family should be the one place where you feel you can be yourself—and be loved for it.
BILL HYBELS

💡 CHALK TALK Write "I love you" or "Welcome Home" with chalk on your driveway or sidewalk to greet a family member.
KATHY PEEL

LAUGH IT UP! Remind your children that what they think is pretty today will change tomorrow. Pull out some of your old photos from those junior high days—especially the bad ones—and let your kids laugh as they look at what you looked like and the ridiculous clothes you wore.

SUSAN ALEXANDER YATES

 DON'T WAIT TO CELEBRATE! Add small embellishments to the ordinary details of life, and turn them into simple celebrations of being alive. Look for everyday happenings to promote—a young child losing her first tooth, a high school senior getting accepted into college, or a spouse closing a big deal.

JUDIE BYRD

 START OFF WITH A SMILE If you're a night owl, this could be a challenge, but give it your best shot. Determine that each morning before they encounter the hostile world, your family will receive a friendly smile from you. *Note: Laughing at their "morning hair" doesn't count!*

LAURA J. BARKER

 FLUFFER UPPER Draw a bath for a family member who's had a hard day. Fluff and warm his or her towel in the dryer.

KATHY PEEL

 LISTEN UP! Healthy families work at active listening. They create windows of opportunity to draw thoughts, feelings, and concerns out of each other. Maybe they do this at the dinner table, at bedtime, or at a Saturday-morning breakfast together. Some families even designate one night a week or one night a month as "family night," so they can really talk to each other.

BILL HYBELS

 FLOWER POWER Send your mother flowers on *your* birthday to thank her for bringing you into the world.

JUDIE BYRD

DO YOU EVER FEEL LIKE A DRILL SERGEANT MOM? YOUR KIDS
walk in the door from school and you hit them with a list of
orders: "Go practice your piano." "Do your homework before
ballet." "Remember to tidy up your room." "Don't forget to call
about baby-sitting.""Hurry up and pick up those toys like I told
you to."

While nagging can't be avoided altogether, here are five things
you can do, compliments of mother-and-child expert Susan
Alexander Yates, to eliminate unnecessary nagging and make
your family life more fun!

Do Some Positive Nagging

SUSAN ALEXANDER YATES

Too much nagging is exhausting and unpleasant for everyone. But surprise! Part of your job as a parent *is* to nag. After
all, your primary goal is to build kids with strong, godly
character—and this takes intentional training and repetition.
Here's how to be a positive nag:

1. Decide what's really important. Where will you be le-
nient—and where will you hang tough? For example, hair
length, faded holey jeans, and untucked big shirts really
aren't worth nagging about. But there are several things
our family is tough on:

- *Thoughtfulness.* We expect our kids to write thank-you
  notes, walk their friends to the door, look adults in the
  eye, and leave the house cleaner than they found it when
  they baby-sit for people. It's a way of honoring others.
- *Responsibility.* We want our kids to grow into responsible, reliable adults. Learning to do things properly
  teaches responsibility. We decrease the necessity of
  nagging when we train our kids carefully *in the beginning.*
- *Self-discipline.* Our kids need to learn life isn't based on

feelings. We go to work whether we feel like it or not. Our kids must do homework whether they feel like it or not.

2. Give clear instructions—and follow through with consequences. Often nagging occurs because someone didn't hear your instructions or misunderstood you. Eliminate this cause of nagging by clearly writing out instructions—and then spelling out specific deadlines and clear consequences for lack of action. For example, at our house, unless thank-you notes are written by a specific time, there is no TV, no use of the car, and no friends over until they are finished. When you follow through, your kids will learn you mean what you say.

3. Practice prevention. When our twins' first high school exams were approaching, I realized we could be headed for an unpleasant couple of weeks of my nagging them about studying. So two weeks before their exams began, we sat down together to develop a study strategy.

The first time we did this, I was very involved. Now that they are juniors in high school, I simply ask them to give me a written copy of their exam study schedules. I look it over, offer a few suggestions, pray for them, encourage them with treats, and try not to nag them to study.

4. Involve the whole family. When you feel as though you've become a constant nag, it's time to have a family discussion. Brainstorm creative ways to resolve the issue. Be sure to be positive. Avoid words such as "you always" or "you never." Instead say, "How can we solve this problem so I don't have to stay on everyone's case?"

5. Maintain a sense of humor. When we laugh at ourselves, we take the sting out of a difficult situation. Be patient. Our kids don't mature overnight, and neither do we. God has a lifetime to develop us. When we keep in mind we're all growing together, we'll nag less and laugh more.

IF YOU'RE FEELING A LITTLE FRAZZLED FROM TOO MUCH running, too little sleep, too many expectations, and too few "you" activities, take time out—for yourself! And don't feel guilty either. God created us all with a need for rest, and we women usually don't get enough of it because we're too busy trying to run the world (I know).

TAKE TIME OUT FOR YOURSELF

The presence of small children who love to be near you can make private time seem impossible. But finding it is crucial to keep from driving yourself and your children crazy. Try these handy tips by Karen Dockrey.

ITSY BITS Appreciate bits of time. Savor those five minutes while your child colors. Know that several little bits of time add up to plentiful refreshment.

R & R Continue rest times even after your children give up naps. Send each child to a separate room for an hour of reading or quiet play in the early afternoon. Use this hour to do what you enjoy best; both you and your child will be ready to enjoy each other after some time apart.

BEDDY-BYE Enforce bedtime. Those first few weeks of teaching our children to stay in their beds at bedtime were exhausting for my husband and me. But now we no longer have to deal with "one more drink of water" or "one more hug." Our children are happier because they know the limits, and we are happier because we have uninterrupted time.

KIDS' EXCHANGE Exchange children with a friend. Trade hours, mornings, or evenings so each of you can have some time alone or with your spouse.

GOOD REMINDER Keep reminding yourself that your children won't be underfoot forever. Children grow up faster than we want them to. Present together times can be precious with bits of peace interspersed.

Aching for some "you" time? Don't wait until you're on the edge of exhaustion. Put time for yourself on your calendar, and don't let it get bumped. Try these fun ideas by Jane Johnson Struck, and then come up with your own!

YOUR CHOICE Rent a video you've been dying to see but know none of your friends or your husband is interested in.

TREASURE HUNT Spend a morning hunting down garage sales to see what low-priced, "just for fun" treasures you can find.

BUBBLY TREAT Break out the bubble bath, take the phone off the hook, and soothe your tensions away.

WALK A MALL Just for fun—take up mall walking! You'll lose pounds, tone up, and window-shop at the same time.

LUNCH AND MUNCH Have a friend you've been dying to catch up with? Schedule a lunch with your friend at the nicest restaurant that's affordable.

WE ALL SCREAM FOR ICE CREAM Treat yourself to an ice-cream cone in an unpredictable flavor.

SCHEDULE A CLASS Have you wished you could golf or snorkel? Now's the time to sign up for classes in something you've always been interested in.

A WALK DOWN MEMORY LANE Pore through old photo albums, children's memorabilia, or college notebooks. What memories they'll invoke!

TIME-SAVER Remember you don't have to say yes to every opportunity. The more time you save, the more you can find for those you love—and yourself.

━━━━━ ━━━━━ ━━━━━ ━━━━━ ━━━━━

WHEN MY FRIEND SANDY TOLD ME SHE WAS REMARRYING, I was thrilled. She'd had a tough time as a single parent after her husband's death, and I knew her husband-to-be, Sam, well. Both Christians, Sandy and Sam were in counseling, along with Sandy's two daughters. "We're thrilled about our upcoming marriage . . . but also scared," Sandy had confided. "It helped when a friend told me blending her family wasn't always easy, but it was worth all the work!"

If you are a stepparent or stepchild, you're dealing with some complicated relationships. But with God's help, some perspective, and a sense of humor, your family can succeed, just like Mayo Mathers in the following story:

Accept the Changes That Stepfamilies Bring to Your Relationships

MAYO MATHERS

At first I'd been thrilled when Mom married Don fifteen years ago. Widowed at thirty-two, she'd committed her life to raising my brother, sister, and me. But all of us kids were married by then, with families of our own, and I was glad she wouldn't be alone anymore.

Don understood the pain of losing a spouse. His wife had died several years earlier, leaving him with three teenage daughters. When Mom and Don announced their plans to marry, both families rejoiced, and at the wedding, all six kids stood up with the bride and groom. It couldn't have been more perfect.

But when Mom said "I do," it brought drastic changes. My brother, sister, and I had been the center of her world. Even as an adult, I drew tremendous strength from this knowledge. Before her marriage to Don, Mom frequently drove the more than three hours to my house. Once my kids were asleep, we'd brew a pot of tea and curl up for homey late-night chats.

Her marriage changed that. Secure in her relationship with

her own children, she concentrated on her relationship with Don and his family. Understanding this didn't make it any easier.

The first time I visited Mom and Don after their wedding, reality set in. Mom had sold her house and moved to Don's dairy farm. Gone was the furniture I'd grown up with, the curios our family had collected, the dishes I'd argued with my sister over washing. The photographs on the wall were of people I didn't know, occasions I hadn't participated in. For the first time, it occurred to me I'd never be able to go "home" again. That place of my heart no longer existed.

The responsibilities of the dairy farm made it impossible for Mom to get away to visit me. And when I went to see her, cozy visiting was just as impossible. Shouting interesting bits of news at her as we fed fifty bawling calves just wasn't the same.

I began to feel orphaned, and Don was the easiest person to blame. I was thirty-five years old and wanted to throw a three-year-old tantrum. I envisioned myself grabbing Don by the throat and screaming, "I want my mother *back!*" "God," I wept into my pillow after one particularly difficult visit, "I miss my mother! Will things ever be the same again?"

Would you prefer she be alone, just so she can be at your beck and call? God countered.

No, I never wished her back to widowhood. But my negative feelings had caught me off guard. I'd expected only minor adjustments with this remarriage, since my brother,

My only regret after Mom's death is that, although I had challenged her to make needed changes in her life, I spent too many years judging her instead of loving her. Now when I have to say challenging and convicting things to others, I try to season my words with love and say them at the right time.

KATHY TROCCOLI

sister, and I were settled into our own lives, as were Don's children. But the collective relatives were seldom together long enough to feel like a family.

As time passed, Mom began adding her own personal touches to the farmhouse. Each time I visited, something familiar from my childhood had found its way into the decor. The lumpy clay pitcher formed by my ten-year-old hands now sat on the kitchen shelf. The wooden bowl carved by my brother was displayed on the coffee table, and my sister's hand-sewn comforter covered the bed in the guest room.

I was especially happy when Mom repapered the kitchen. The room had been decorated around the garish orange and green of the sixties, and I loved the softer color scheme Mom chose.

Don's daughters, however, weren't as enthusiastic about the new kitchen when they came home to visit. At first I didn't understand their reaction and felt they weren't giving Mom a fair chance. But as I prayed about this, God helped me see these changes through my stepsisters' eyes.

I realized as Mom put out familiar objects from our family, some of their family disappeared. The kitchen I thought looked so pretty now had been lovingly decorated by their mother. To them it must have felt as if her personality had been ripped from the room along with their yellowed paper.

Although every change Mom made in the farmhouse made it feel more familiar, one Christmas my brother, sister, and I discussed the possibility of having Christmas at one of our homes instead of at the farm, where the dinner and gift exchange had to be squeezed in among endless chores.

Astoundingly, the suggestion met with loud protests from all our children: "It won't be like Christmas if we're not at the farm!"

As I listened to their complaints, one thing became very clear. The farm might not feel like home to me, but it was home to the grandkids. This was the only house they could remember Grandma living in, and it was as much a part of their heritage as our grandmother's house was to us.

That realization—more than anything else—made the line between our family and Don's family soften in my eyes. Knowing my children saw everyone simply as their family made all the difference.

The greatest proof of all came last Thanksgiving. Once again the two families were crowded around a bountiful table, knees touching, elbows bumping— but there were no longer knots in my stomach. And, as usual, Don signaled for us to hold hands as we prayed. My son Tyler, now a teenager, sat calmly. However two-year-old Levi, son of my stepsister, Danise, soon wearied of his grandpa's prayer. I could sense Danise's growing tension. How well I remembered the days of having the only toddler at the table!

Just as Don brought his prayer to an end, Levi banged his fork loudly against his plate, startling Tyler with the noise. As Levi laughed in delight, Tyler looked at me and grinned. "I'm never having kids!" he stated.

My parents always made me feel welcome. They were never too busy to give me attention. Even as a teenager, I thought I must be the most entertaining company in the world because my folks loved to be with me—and with each of my siblings. It didn't occur to me until later that they chose to spend time with us.

TWILA PARIS

I laughed, remembering when those same words were spoken in response to him, and looked at the faces circling the table. When Mom married Don, time didn't stop for me to adjust to the changes. It kept moving forward, and I had the choice to move with it or be dragged along in the dust. Even though I'd spent much of that time digging my heels firmly into the past, a miracle had been unfolding. All the while, the people gathered around this table were being transformed from acquaintances to relatives to family. My family.

DIRTY DIAPERS. TOYS STREWN FROM ROOM TO ROOM.
Mismatched socks and half-drunk glasses of milk. Muddy
footprints on the kitchen floor and even muddier jeans from
playing football in the rain with friends. Not being able to use the
phone, even when you purchased a second line.

If you're a parent, you can identify with the above list of
woes. Sometimes in our frustration with the "dailies" of parenting, it's easy to see kids as problems instead of "precious." If
you've ever felt like running away from parenthood, meet someone who did—and read about what she learned.

Realize Children *Do* Grow Up

FAYE ROBERTS

My hands gripped the steering wheel of my brown station
wagon as it careened past the lush lawns, trimmed hedges,
and flower beds of my neighborhood. As its fender came
dangerously close to a curbside garbage can, I groaned,
remembering it was trash day—and mine was still in a heap
in the garage. Then it dawned on me: It didn't matter. I was
running away!

It was the middle of summer vacation, and I had four bored
kids—even though, for the last six weeks, I had driven them to
endless softball games, piano and tennis lessons, orthodontist
appointments, and trips to the pool. I had survived slumber
parties, backyard campouts, melting Popsicles, loud music,
and fights over the bathroom. I had been available for all
emergencies—bike wrecks, cut fingers, splinters, broken
hearts, and disputes over whose night it was to do the dishes or
feed the dog and who got the last ice-cream bar.

I was sick of nagging my kids to clean up their rooms, turn
down the stereo, put their cereal bowls in the sink, quit
arguing, and not lean back in their chairs. I was tired of being
motherly! I yearned for adventure.

I swerved onto the highway and headed south. Sunglasses

on, I sang loudly to the Beatles' tune on the oldies station, my salt-and-pepper hair flying in the wind and feet dancing on the floorboard. When the sign for a fast-food restaurant waved me in, I ordered a double cheeseburger with bacon, onion rings, and a chocolate-banana shake—throwing my sensible diet out the window of my Subaru.

As I reached in my billfold to pay at the drive-up window, a prayer card fluttered into my lap. "Love is patient, love is kind," the card read. "It does not envy, it does not boast, it is not proud. It is not rude, it is not self-seeking, it is not easily angered, it keeps no record of wrongs" (1 Cor. 13:4-5).

As I parked the car and unwrapped my burger, those words played in my mind like a recurring song. *What did the apostle Paul know,* I thought. *He never had four bored kids!* But as I ate my burger and slurped down the last of my shake, the melody of the words gently eased my frustration.

I glanced at my watch. Mandy's piano lesson was at 5 P.M. Amy had a game at 5:30. I needed to move on! As I put my billfold back in my purse and glanced at the faded picture of smiling cherub faces, I whispered, "Thank you, Lord, for these people you've put in my care. Give me patience." Then I headed north, toward home, with the melody playing on.

THINK IT OVER
Mother and child-expert Susan Alexander Yates says, "Our family doesn't need us to be perfect—but they do need to see us striving to live out our faith. And that calls for us to be humble, consistent, trustworthy, and honest in our daily lives." What's one way you can "live out your faith" more consistently with your family this week?

Finances

Who isn't tempted by material things?
But when I am, I ask myself, What's more
important—my relationship with God, or these
temporary things? That always gives me perspective.

CeCe Winans

ARE YOU FINANCIALLY SECURE?

IF there's anything I have a love/hate relationship with, it's money. I love money because it buys what my family and I need. And I'm especially grateful when I can use it creatively to meet others' needs. But I also hate money because all of us inherently have the drive for "more, more, more." It's tough living in a materialistic world where we are constantly bombarded with purchases that, according to advertisers, will "make our life better." So what's the answer?

We can't stick our head in the sand and pretend that money isn't important. For, as the great mystery novelist Agatha Christie said, "Those who never think about money need a great deal of it!" Instead, we need to realize that we're being tempted by the world's lie by thinking that acquiring more money will make us happy. And then we can make well-informed choices about how to spend the money God *has* given us. That's what this chapter is all about.

HAVE YOU EVER LOOKED AT A FRIEND AND WISHED

- you had her job instead of yours?
- your house looked like hers—clutter-free and beautifully decorated?
- your kids were well-behaved, too, when your in-laws come over?
- you had a husband who gave you romantic surprises like hers?

If you have, you're not alone. All of us, at one time or another, wish for more out of life. Here's what one woman discovered about living in a "never enough" world.

Be Content with What You Have

R. RUTH BARTON

When my husband and I were first married and lived in a small apartment, I thought if we could just buy a house I'd be satisfied.

Several years later, we did get our house. Even though it was a modest, three-bedroom ranch in need of decorating and repair, it felt so good to have space! And to walk out our front door into a grassy yard rather than a dank hallway seemed like heaven on earth. For the privilege of owning a home I could certainly live with peeling paint, yellow-and-green wallpaper, and an outdated kitchen.

Or could I?

It didn't take long for me to realize I'm not that easily satisfied. Oh, I was fine as long as the first flush of purchasing excitement lasted. But pretty soon, desire began to overtake me again. If we could just replace the shag carpeting, get rid of the avocado appliances, remodel the kitchen . . . then I'd be satisfied.

Well, here it is ten years later. We've done all those things (and more!) and I've made a startling realization: It doesn't matter how much we buy, there is always plenty more that I want.

EXPOSING THE MYTHS

In this never-enough world, the myth of materialism is preached as though it were the gospel truth. Nearly every time we open a magazine, turn on the television, or talk to a neighbor, we're bombarded with the message that material things provide the answers to life's basic questions. What am I worth? The most expensive hair color. What is success? Having an American Express card. How do I find peace of mind? Buy more insurance. How do I show someone how much I love them? Send a Hallmark card. And what do I do when the going gets tough? Go shopping, of course.

Materialism promises that if we can just achieve a higher income level, get our dream house, wear the right clothes, and enjoy the right kinds of leisure activities, we will be satisfied. But in reality, it often produces families that are unable to get off the treadmill because they are deeply in debt; parents who have no time for each other or their children; men and women who know how to dress for success but are full of doubts and questions on the inside.

For years I was consumed by money, prestige, recognition.

I ended up with broken relationships, a fractured family life, and spiritual drought. Now I've chosen to be consumed by God's Spirit and his will. There's no question in my mind I've finally made the right choice.

ATHENA DEAN

THE SOURCE OF OUR DISCONTENT

As much as I'm influenced by cultural expectations, I'm learning that the source of my discontent goes far deeper than that. I'm most vulnerable when I drift from the relationships for which I was created.

When sin, rebellion, or lack of attention causes a rift in our most important relationship—with God—the resulting emptiness of soul can be very painful. Although we may try to fill our emptiness by acquiring more things, make no mistake about it: There'll never be enough material things to satisfy the longings of the human soul. That's why the book of Hebrews draws such a strong connection between freedom from materialism and our relationship with God: "Keep your lives free from the love of money and be content with what you have, because God has said, 'Never will I leave you; never will I forsake you'" (13:5). The questions that the myth of materialism claim to answer can only be satisfied in a personal relationship with the Lord. The more consistent we are in pursuing that relationship, the less obsessed we'll be with money and things.

KEEPING THINGS IN PERSPECTIVE

I'd be unrealistic if I didn't admit how much I enjoy the things money buys. Our home with its grassy lawn and good neighbors has been a wonderful place to raise our family and host our friends. My newly remodeled kitchen is saving me untold time and frustration so I'm free to devote more time to people and activities that really interest me. And life would certainly be more difficult without adequate, regular income. I enjoy these gifts without guilt because God "richly provides us with everything for our enjoyment" (1 Tim. 6:17).

But a balanced perspective reminds me that money does have its limitations. It can buy clothes but not true beauty. An exotic vacation but not the ability to relax and sleep. A big house but not a happy family. Sports fees and equipment but not a dad. Expensive gifts but not love. A *Better Homes and Gardens* lifestyle but not a mom who has time and energy left to play games or read stories.

A balanced perspective also keeps me from being consumed by my desires and warns me about sacrificing what really matters in life for things that never quite satisfy. Contrary to the myth of materialism, it isn't the ones who die with the most toys who win. It's those who've loved their families well and know the joy of having that love returned. It's those who've known what it is to spend their lives for a purpose greater than themselves. It's those who've known their God and look forward to eternity with him.

Attitude is more important than the past, than education, than money, than circumstances. Every day we have a choice regarding the attitude we will embrace for that day.

CHARLES SWINDOLL

ASKING THE RIGHT QUESTIONS

Oftentimes, the questions we ask ourselves are just as important as the answers we think we know. In fact, I've found that the process of asking questions is the answer to my struggle with cultural influences, great expectations, and emptiness of soul: What do I expect out of life, and where do those expectations come from? What is success, and do I tend to measure it by outward trappings? How much of myself am I giving to my loved ones, and how much am I relying on expensive gifts (for birthdays or Christmas, for example) to communicate love? What is the real source of the emptiness or drivenness I feel?

In the noisiness of daily life, it's hard to quiet ourselves and wait for the answers to questions that are as important as these. But answers that fit into simple categories of right and wrong or 1-2-3 solutions are not the ones we're looking for. Real answers offer us insights about ourselves, the material world, and the spiritual world, and free us to choose a lifestyle consistent with our core values rather than cultural myths. Real answers help us keep our perspective in a world where desire is out of control. Real answers take us deeper into the relationships for which we were created. And it's only then that we'll be satisfied.

HAVE YOU EVER SPENT AN AFTERNOON AT THE MALL AND returned home with an armful of purchases? Chances are, you enjoyed it, but what about the credit-card bill that came a month later? In this "buy, buy" world, it's tempting to spend beyond our budget. If you're looking for ways to curb your spending habits without total mall withdrawal, read on for some great ideas.

Curb Compulsive Spending

DEBRA PETROSKY

"Soon after getting my first job, my spending spun wildly out of control," Natalie admitted. "With all major charge cards safely tucked in my wallet, I spent my lunch hours shopping at downtown department stores. If I needed a skirt, I came home with a new blouse, too. By using my plastic money at a furious rate and making only minimum payments, I soon racked up three thousand dollars in bills. If you added my car loan, my debt totaled nearly seven thousand dollars."

Natalie worked six years to pay off her debts before getting married. How did she break her compulsive spending habits? Here are some ideas:

1. Don't read the ads unless you know you need something. Clever advertisers create a felt need with enticing color, creative ad copy, and airbrushed beauty. Are you buying steak or just the sizzle?

2. Do you have an impulse to buy something stylish, chic, or expensive? Wait two weeks and see if you still want it. Use that time to comparison shop, especially for big-ticket items.

3. Always shop with a list—and stick to it. Keep a notebook with your family's sizes and upcoming clothing needs. If you discover a terrific sale, you can take advantage of the bargain without feeling guilty.

4. Have a plan when you shop for clothes. Does that sharp dress fit your color scheme and the accessories you already have? If you buy it, will you also need new shoes, a purse, and earrings to make your outfit complete?

5. Look at the cost of items in terms of your wage. If you're earning $7 an hour, that snazzy pair of leather pumps will cost you the equivalent of a day's wage. When you think of your purchase in those terms, is it really worth that much to you?

6. If the mall is a stumbling block for you, don't meet friends there for fellowship. Choose a restaurant, a park, or the tennis courts instead.

7. Do you have to buy the item new, or will used do? Check with relatives, friends, and the classified ads for a good deal. Do you know someone who's an avid garage saler? Tag along for the experience of shopping for a bargain.

8. Can you repair existing goods instead of sinking money into new ones? Getting a comfortable pair of shoes resoled is less expensive than buying new ones. Ask a seamstress about altering that suit so you don't have to buy a new one.

9. Use cash or write checks instead of charging it. If you write a check, record your purchase immediately and compute your new balance. If you must use a charge card, determine to pay off your balance each month.

10. Finally, don't forget to pray. Time in God's presence will also help you discern the difference between needs and wants—a key to curbing compulsive spending.

WHEN WE ASKED TCW READERS ACROSS THE COUNTRY TO share their best money-saving tips, we were deluged with a flurry of frugal finds. So before your next trip to the grocery store or the mall, check out these thrifty tips. They just may save you some money!

MAKE THE MOST OF YOUR MONEY

 FRUGAL FOOD Instead of going out to dinner, just go out for dessert or a cup of coffee. It's a fun way to get out without the high cost.

MARY K. CALAWA

 CHEAP CHIC Attend rummage sales and thrift stores—especially in the wealthier parts of town. You can get some really great deals on brand-name clothing. Keep a list in your purse of each family member's size.

KRISTI KRAMLICH-KUBALL

 CLEAN AND THRIFTY I cut laundry expenses by buying detergent from a laundromat. The fifty-pound box for thirty-seven dollars lasts half a year for our family of four. I tear dryer sheets in half and reuse them until there is no more fragrance. Instead of buying stain-remover sticks and liquids, I use a nail brush to scrub a little cheap shampoo or dish detergent into grimy collars and grassy knees.

JEANNE ZORNES

 SEED SAVVY I love gardening and could easily spend large sums of money during planting season every spring. But rather than pay exorbitant amounts at the nursery, I let some of my annual flowers go to seed every summer. I collect the seeds, dry them, store them in labeled small plastic bags, and save them for the following spring. I also swap my perennials and herbs with family and friends. We each increase the variety of flowers and plants in our gardens without increasing the cost. And we add beauty to God's green earth.

JOAN MARIE ARBOGAST

DON'T FORGET TO BORROW For parties and evening wear, I often borrow a dress from a same-size friend (and return it dry cleaned). If shoes are needed to go with it, I go to the local discount shoe outlet. Shoes don't need to be high quality if they aren't worn often.

DENISE A. VEZEY

SMART STATIONERY We save money on stationery by making it ourselves. The kids make their own thank-you notes by decorating the waste sheets of perforated computer paper that my husband brings home from work. Stamps, markers, and a little creativity can yield something fancier.

SUSAN PEISKER

HOLIDAY HINTS After-holiday candy sales are almost give-aways. Most candy freezes well and can be used for other holidays, parties, baking, stocking stuffers, and movie snacks.

LETTIE J. KIRKPATRICK

HOUSE OF BARGAINS We started paying fifty dollars extra on our monthly house payments—a separate check marked "for principal only"—and are saving a tremendous amount of money in the long run by reducing our interest payments.

MARLA SHIREY

WISE BUYS I put myself on a daily cash allowance. If I run out of cash, that's it for the day. The most important thing I've done to save money is to ask God to help me be more frugal. The more I depend on his wisdom in money matters instead of my own, the less I struggle in this area.

LIZ HELLER

BARTERING—THE EXCHANGE OF ONE SERVICE FOR ANOTHER without the use of money—has been around for centuries. But with today's tough economic times, women around the country are rediscovering bartering as an effective—and fun—way to cut costs, save money, and utilize the skills and resources they have at their fingertips. Maybe it's time for *you* to try it out!

Bartering Is Better

KAY DEKALB SMITH

When my husband and I discovered it was impossible to fit piano lessons for our seven-year-old daughter into our budget, my mind started to race: *Could there be a way to "pay" for piano lessons that didn't involve money?*

Several days later I called a local piano teacher, explained our situation, and asked her if she'd be open to other payment options. We agreed that for every new student I brought to her, my daughter could have a month's free lessons. The result? After some creative advertising and work on my part, the piano teacher got twelve new students, and I got a year's free lessons. We were both thrilled to have our needs met without having to spend any money.

Another woman I know got her car repaired in exchange for calling the garage's customers with past-due accounts. And my friend Emily used her knack for sewing to make kitchen curtains in exchange for homemade frozen pies.

If you're interested in venturing into the world of bartering, here's how to begin.

1. Make a list. Jot down your needs, goals, and aspirations. Then list what you have to swap. Don't limit yourself to personal skills or abilities. Do you have freezer space, a garden plow, a sewing machine, a food processor, even an extra bedroom? My grandmother lets her neighbor store things in her garage, and he mows her grass all summer. My friend Dottie lets me borrow her card tables when I entertain, and I get her mail when she travels.

2. Advertise. Once you've hit on what you're able to offer in exchange for a particular service, advertise. A church newsletter or local newspaper is a great place to start. Or set up a "barter board" at your apartment complex, workplace, church office, grocery store, or school. Clearly state your need and what you have to offer in exchange.

3. Don't be shy. Did you know that some businesses barter? If you need dental work or are behind in your rent, why not ask to barter apartment cleaning, lawn care, phone answering, snow shoveling, litter removal, pool vacuuming, or painting? Also, share the idea of bartering in the small groups you are already involved in: Sunday school class, garden club, or homeschoolers. Brainstorm about needs and creative options for meeting those needs.

4. Be sensitive. Bartering is good, but sometimes the possessions you have are not to be bartered but freely given. Only you can determine what God would have you do. Perhaps you have observed a need but know that person doesn't want "charity." In one such case, I offered a family some desperately needed cash in exchange for washing my windows. Ultimately, we are commanded to be wise stewards of all our God-given resources. After all, everything we have is God's (Psalm 50:10-11). Bartering is just a creative way to spread it all around!

MY FRIEND ANN IS ONE OF THE WORLD'S GREATEST SUPER savers. If I want to know where to find a good quality item at a discount price, I just call her. As a single parent of two young children, she's learned, out of necessity, how to save money— and have fun doing it. If you're looking for some strategies to save money, read on. And then add your own!

STRATEGIZE FOR SUPER SAVING

KEEP YOUR EYES ON SALES Each week, review ads from local grocery and drug/discount stores, make a list of sale items that interest you, and pull one coupon for each purchase. Whenever possible, buy bulk quantities—you will rarely pay full price.

KIMBERLY MALKOGAINNIS

POCKETBOOK EMPTY? Don't give up on providing special gifts for friends and family just because you're a little low on cash. Instead, give gifts of time. Baby-sit for a new mom who needs a night off; make cookies for a neighbor who's having a tough time; sew curtains for a single friend who's moving into an apartment; make a family video and send it to distant loved ones. Brainstorm your own ideas, based on your time and talent, and then surprise your loved one!

RAE CARMEN

DISCOUNT WATCH Watch for markdowns. While many discounters claim they never stage "sales," they often reduce prices more than once to keep their merchandise moving out of the store.

SARA NELSON

BASIC BUYING Keep emergency meal supplies in your pantry (pasta, rice, tomato sauce, or whatever you regularly eat), your fridge (milk, bread, cheese), and freezer (hamburger, chicken) for a minimum of three meals

for your family. That way you'll never be caught with
having to go out for a meal when you can't afford it just
because there's nothing to eat!

CANDACE BREMEN

 BARGAIN SENSE Don't buy any clothes item unless you
- really need (and don't just want) it;
- it fits;
- it's in your price range.

A bargain isn't a bargain unless you can afford it and
you end up wearing it a year from now.

LAURA CRANDALL

 WATER'S GOOD FOR YOU—AND YOUR POCKETBOOK When
you dine out, save money by using restaurant coupons and
choosing water as a beverage.

KIMBERLY MALKOGAINNIS

 REFUND-O-MANIA To save extra money on purchases, shop
at a store that offers both good prices and coupon
"doubling." Highlight expiration dates on coupons and
organize them in a coupon keeper.

ELIZABETH WOLF

 BE A STASH SHOPPER Having to look for birthday, holiday,
and baby gifts on short notice? I've solved this problem by
checking every sale table for gift possibilities and buying
several. Then when my child comes home Thursday with a
weekend party invitation, she goes to the closet to pick out a
gift from my stash—and I save myself a mad dash to the
store.

KAREN DOCKREY

 KNOW WHEN TO SAY "ENOUGH IS ENOUGH!" When I go
shopping, I evaluate what I'm purchasing: Is it a necessity,
or could my money be used for a more valuable purpose
such as to feed the hungry or clothe the poor?

JODY HILL

ASK ANY MARRIAGE COUNSELOR WHAT THE TOP THREE
issues of discussion are, and you're sure to hear "money" among
the list. Why money? Most marriage partners come from varying
financial backgrounds: One may be frugal, never spending
money on herself/himself, while the other has expensive hobbies;
one may hold on tightly to money, while the other gives it away
freely; one may have significant business experience, while the
other has never balanced a checkbook. But whatever your
background, as you and your spouse (or potential spouse) discuss
your financial future, here's a checklist to keep in mind.

Discuss Financial Responsibility with Your Spouse

JANIS LONG HARRIS

As newlyweds, my husband, Paul, and I wanted to avoid the
friction we'd been warned could result from disagreements
over money since money issues tap into so many sensitive
areas in marriage—power, control, self-esteem, gender
roles, and spiritual values.

When we asked some of our married friends, we discovered many creative solutions to our dilemma. While there's
no one right way to approach family management, there are
some guidelines for deciding what approach to take in div-
vying up financial tasks and decision making. The following
questions may help you as you consider what might work
best for you and your spouse:

WHO LIKES TO DO IT?

When you're trying to decide on a workable division of
financial labor, it's important to consider your own and your
spouse's natural gifts and preferences. If one spouse is particularly talented at or interested in money management, that
person might want to take on a larger role.

My friend Carolyn, for example, is an at-home mom who thrives on managing her family's finances. She makes most purchases, pays bills, balances the checkbook, and oversees an aggressive investment program. She continues to be an avid reader of books and articles about finance and has been successful in improving the return on their investment. The satisfaction Carolyn feels about her financial role comes from her natural affinity for working with numbers, her ability to take measured risks, and her husband's appreciation for what she's doing.

Although the Bible doesn't address a "Christian" way to shop, God makes it clear he expects us to invest wisely in ways that reap returns for his kingdom. For me, that means carving out time with my family and controlling my spending.

JANE JOHNSON STRUCK

"Mark encourages me to take an active role in setting and pursuing financial goals for our family because he doesn't have the interest or personality for it," says Carolyn.

Although my friend Paula's husband handles their checkbook and pays all the bills, she does their tax return and takes care of all insurance matters. "I enjoy figuring out our taxes," she explains, "and I'm the one who knows what all our insurance coverages are and when we're getting a good deal."

Sherry, on the other hand, does all the routine bill-paying while her husband has an annual "encounter" with their taxes.

Sylvie handles virtually all money-management tasks in her marriage because she has more experience with finances than her husband, who never had a credit card until they were married. "When our checkbook balances to the penny, it makes me feel like life is in order," she says with a happy sigh.

WHO HAS THE TIME?

Some couples divvy up money chores according to who has the most time or schedule flexibility to accommodate the job. "I hate paying the bills," says Robin, "but my husband works such long hours that it would be a huge ordeal for him to pay them."

Other couples try to lighten the burden by sharing it. Tina and Paul take turns handling the finances—she does it one year and he does it the next. Mona and Jim cut down on the time they'd have to expend to pay all the family bills by each doing part. They keep separate checking accounts and a joint savings account. Jim pays the house mortgage, and Mona pays the other bills. They both contribute a set amount to their savings.

Lynnette and Curt play it by ear—whoever has the most open schedule when it's time to pay the bills or balance the checkbook takes care of it.

WHO IS MOST AFFECTED BY IT?

Many women say managing the checkbook makes sense when they're the ones making most of the day-to-day purchasing decisions. Heidi, for example, says she buys most of the groceries, clothing, and household items for her family, so handling the checkbook gives her a degree of flexibility that's important to her.

Sue, on the other hand, has taken on the money-management role because her husband is too inclined to worry about it. "Tom feels the stress of bringing in most of the income," she explains, "so I feel it's only fair for me to have the stress of figuring out how to balance the accounts."

DIVIDING UP YOUR FINANCIAL TURF

In talking with couples about their approaches to money management, I found the most effective systems gave both spouses a sense of individual control over how money is spent. There are several ways to do that. Paula and her husband, for example, have agreed on areas of primary decision making. Paula's domain is the household, so she makes all money decisions related to it. Her husband is the primary financial decision maker in other areas. Any major purchases or money decisions are discussed together.

Other couples achieve a sense of individual control by dividing up spending money—each partner has a certain amount to spend as he or she pleases.

THE ACCOUNTABILITY FACTOR

Every couple needs to discuss major money decisions, even when they've divided up their financial roles or monetary turf. One simple way to handle the accountability issue is to stipulate an amount—say two hundred dollars—and agree that neither of you will make a purchase or financial commitment involving that amount or more without consulting the other.

God's principles of finances are not an arbitrary set of rules by which to govern us; they are a loving Father's wisdom to those who will listen and trust him.

LARRY BURKETT

One of the most important keys to a conflict-free approach to money management in marriage seems to be a couple's basic attitude towards money. If money is a symbol of power, is equated with success, or is viewed as a necessary component of a couple's dreams, it almost certainly is going to be a destructive force in marriage.

Who should mind the money in your marriage? That answer will depend on several criteria, including who has a natural affinity for managing it, who has the time, who is most affected by it, and how much need you and your husband have for a sense of individual control. You have to craft an approach that best fits your temperaments, lifestyle, and ability to discipline yourselves.

While there's no one right answer to the question of who should manage the money in a given family, it's important that spouses agree on—and affirm each other for—their respective roles. Those roles may change over time as jobs, circumstances, and priorities shift. But as long as couples work together, understand their gifts, and seek to be good stewards of the financial resources God has blessed them with, it's likely their money will be managed well.

HAVE YOU RECENTLY LOST YOUR JOB? ARE YOU LOW ON cash and high on college loans after graduation? Have you experienced a personal crisis that has sapped your financial resources? Are you tired of the daily grind of long work hours and still not making enough money for your family's needs?

If you're feeling discouraged, remember, you're not alone. God has promised to walk through the tough times with you if you'll trust him for the outcome. And, as the following story relates, you'll make a surprising discovery—that there's *always* something to be thankful for, no matter what your circumstances.

Be Thankful Even in Tough Times

SUSAN M. BAILEY

After switching from a part-time office job to at-home freelance work, my income dropped significantly. My husband Richard's sales job for a new housing project was not bringing in the money we thought it would. And our three young sons' needs for clothing, food, and other essentials were increasing faster than our ability to keep pace.

For us, money became more than just a question of how to make ends meet—it became a spiritual issue. Was God really able to provide for us as he promises in the Bible?

Needing God's assurance, I studied my Bible for evidences of God's provision. Almost every passage I read seemed to be about trusting God, believing that he is in control. As characters in the Bible obeyed God in faith, they were blessed abundantly. As I began to trust God more and grew more dependent on him, he was able to use our scarcity to teach me these critical lessons.

Seek first the kingdom. Jesus understood our tendency to be more concerned about the essentials of this world than about eternity. Yet over and over in Scripture, he chides us for worrying about what we eat, drink, and wear. When fretting about tomorrow began to take away my joy, I resolved to make Luke 12:22-34 my personal wake-up call. Each morning I read these verses and ask God to help me see his provision during the day. Then at bedtime, I take a few minutes to review the day and praise God for his many blessings.

Pray always and about everything. I used to be uncomfortable praying for "insignificant" things like utility payments. But now I bring *every* concern before the Lord. In return he's blessed me with a spirit of calmness that is not my own (Phil. 4:6-7).

Seek support. Even when we give our burdens to Jesus and trust in his provision, we may still carry some residual fear. Share your worries with someone who will pray for you and help you see God's provision from an objective viewpoint.

Be good to yourself. When the pressure is on, don't neglect yourself. I try to walk, read, nap, listen to music, pray, or read Scripture—anything that restores my energy and takes my mind off my troubles.

Maintain order. Financial uncertainty can leave you feeling as though every aspect of your life is out of control. To counter this stressful lifestyle, keep your home organized by cutting through clutter.

Trust God. Downscaling our lifestyle has become an important spiritual discipline. Through it, my husband and I have learned to trust in God's provision. We've come to see our circumstances as an opportunity to grow in the Lord (Heb. 12:7, 11)—and we know that all we really need, we have in Jesus.

THINK IT OVER
Financial expert and author Ron Blue has said, "Money is not only a tool, but also a test." If you were to give yourself an A, B, C, D, or F on your "Money Report Card" today, what grade would you receive? What steps can you take this week, and in the future, to ensure your financial security?

Friendship

We are the hands and feet of Christ. We need to
do what Christ would do. If people are hungry,
feed them. If they're lonely, talk to them.
If they're discouraged, encourage them. Do it by
whatever means you can—if you can bake, take
them some banana bread. If you can read, then go
and read. Do what you can to make a
difference in somebody's life—one life
at a time, right here at home.

BABBIE MASON

What Season of Friendship Are You In?

SHE'S the one who walked to school with you every day in first grade, who stood up for you when you were being teased in junior high, who talked with you for hours on the phone in high school. She's the loyal soul who helped you through your first breakup, who was a bridesmaid at your wedding, who helped when your son was born. She's the one you fought with, made up with, and would do anything for. Why? Because she's your *friend,* and you couldn't imagine life without her.

But as the seasons of our life change, our friendships will also change. How do you know which ones to hold on to and which ones to let go? How do we find a friend if we're lonely? How can we help a friend who's hurting? How can we become the type of person others want to hang around?

These questions, and many others, are ones we'll address in this chapter.

HOW GLAD I AM THAT, EVEN DURING MY BUSY COLLEGE and early career years, I took time to "make new friends and keep the old," as the song says. Although my three college roommates and I now live in different states (and one even in a different country!), we stay close through visits, phone calls, and E-mail. Over the past seventeen years we've cried together, laughed together, and ridden this wonderful-but-tough ride of friendship together. And through it all, we've learned more about life, God, each other, and ourselves.

In your busy world, do you make time for friends? Here's why you should.

Make Time for Friends—They're Good for You!

DEE BRESTIN

Little girls demand an intimacy in their friendships most boys prefer living without. One day nine-year-old Jonathan told his mother, "Our school bus is so empty we each have a whole seat to ourselves. But the girls are so dumb—they squeeze together on one seat!"

As women, our need for "best friends" rarely changes. But it is also true that today's woman finds it more difficult to maintain friendships. With obvious stress, one woman said, "I'm up at five to pick up the house and fix lunches. I'm at work from eight to four. Then there's laundry, dinner, dishes—and I collapse. I feel guilty that I'm not with my kids more. You tell me when I have time for friends!"

Other women back away from friendship because of hurt. Maybe a friend betrays you, suffocates you, or moves away, and you wonder if friendship is really worth it. It is—and here's why.

WOMEN NEED WOMEN

A recent *Family Circle* study of fifteen thousand women revealed that 69 percent surveyed would rather talk to their best friends than to their husbands when they are unhappy. Women have the ability not only to comfort but also to empathize. Sometimes only another woman can uniquely understand our circumstances.

Julie Hines, a young mother now living in Ohio, tells of a crisis she faced when she was pregnant and on the mission field in Italy. An ultrasound revealed her baby would be born with spina bifida. She and her husband made immediate plans to fly back to the United States to be near friends and family. But on the way to the airport, Julie's water broke. They returned to the hospital for the birth of their daughter, who faced multiple surgeries.

God knows we need a human touch, so he sends people to us— friends who listen, share their stories, and teach us to laugh at ourselves.

SUSAN ASHTON

"I called my best friend, Suzanne, back home," Julie says. "She and her mother arranged for Suzanne to fly over. I'll never forget our meeting in the airport. It was as though there was a physical lightening of my load. Although my husband was wonderful, I needed Suzanne—somehow, she was able to comfort me as only a woman can."

I cannot count the number of times I have been strengthened by another woman's heartfelt hug, appreciative note, surprise gift, or caring question. My women friends are an oasis to me, an encouragement. They are essential to my well-being.

It is only when we appreciate what a gift our women friends are that we will make the effort to overcome the obstacles that threaten friendship's survival.

OVERCOMING STRESS

In today's world, women juggle many roles. Often it seems easiest, when we're under stress, to let friendships go. But it is vital to realize that cutting out friends, especially soul mates, increases rather than decreases stress. Some women who withdraw from friends end up spending time in a counselor's office.

But many women squeeze in time for friends by creatively combining them with necessary tasks. Cindy, a single parent, says, "Another single parent and I take turns cooking for each other once a week. An inviolable rule: Keep it simple! Scrambled eggs or grilled cheese. The kids entertain each other, and Pam and I talk."

"Now that I'm working full-time," Allison shares, "I and six other women bring our brown-bag lunches to the office basement on Thursdays. We share Scripture, our lives, and often tears and hugs—all in less than sixty minutes. That's healing, restorative time—making it possible for us to go back upstairs and finish the day!"

Audrey explains, "About once a month my friend Ginnie and I meet in one of our kitchens and cook double batches of our favorite recipes. This month we made low-calorie spinach lasagna and chicken cacciatore. I can feed my family on that four times!"

My friend Jean and I live four blocks from each other. Several times a week one of us will call the other and ask, "Is this a good time for a walk?" We dash for our Reeboks and meet. We talk about whatever is uppermost on our heart and then pray. Our walks are just long enough to raise our heart rates and our spirits!

OVERCOMING DISTANCE

When a close friend moves away, despite our best intentions, usually phone calls, letters, and prayers wane. Since I have lived in eight states, I cannot possibly stay in touch with all the friends who have been dear to me.

Three years ago I asked myself, "With whom, despite the separation of miles and years, do I still share a bond?" And, "Has she demonstrated a desire to be faithful to me?" Then I prayerfully decided on four long-distance women friends to whom I remain true. I stay in touch at Christmas, on birthdays, and at least one other time a year. It doesn't take a lot of time to write notes, but it does take commitment. I pray for these women's specific needs frequently. It's been a tremendous encouragement to see how the Lord has made visits possible with each one, despite the fact that our homes are spread across the United States.

OVERCOMING BETRAYAL

Lillian Rubin, in *Just Friends,* quotes a nurse who says, "A good warm friendship, like a good warm fire, needs continual stoking." But if you've been hurt, you don't feel like stoking. Many of us forget the warmth and beauty a friendship has given us in the past, concentrate only on our burn, and lay the poker down. The result? The fire dies.

I, like many Christian women, am not a good forgiver. I forgive halfway. When I'm hurt, I don't retaliate but tend to withdraw rather than treat the person as though she never wronged me. The Lord convicted me of my unforgiving attitude toward a friend recently by reminding me of Christ's example of unfailing love. This, and

I try to look at each relationship I'm in—whether it's short-term or long-term—and pray, "Lord, what would you have me say?" I might sow a seed, I might be water, or I might be the harvester. I try to determine by my questions and how they answer what role I could take to bring them one step closer to God.

BECKY TIRABASSI

fear of his discipline, led me to call that friend, telling her the reasons I cherished our friendship. With prayer and persistence, I stoked the dying embers. One day I saw a small flame, then another. Soon, the fires burned brightly again. This friendship now is lovelier than before the breach—because it survived the hardest test.

There will be times when it seems easier to let the flame of friendship die—because we've been genuinely hurt, we're under stress, or because we lack discipline. But friendship is a precious gift. It's well worth the effort required to keep the friends God has given us.

HAVING FRIENDS IS ONE OF THE GREAT JOYS OF LIFE, BUT friendships change as people and circumstances change. Still, as Janis Long Harris and many other women have discovered, it *is* possible—with some effort, intentionality, and a bit of grace—to have satisfying friendships throughout the seasons of life. If you need a friend, here's how to find one, wherever you are!

Realize Friends May Change with Seasons of Life
JANIS LONG HARRIS

My college years were a period of intense friendships. My dorm mates and I often stayed up late, talking about our questions, hopes, dreams, and disappointments. We played good-natured practical jokes, giggled endlessly, and contemplated the meaning of life. We shared our clothes, french fries, and spiritual journeys.

Then came graduation. As a young career woman, I suddenly found I had to *work* at my friendships. Even my apartment mates couldn't be taken for granted as automatic friends, because our lives and schedules were so different. I had to learn to be intentional about my friendships, to initiate activities.

Whether you're single, married, with or without children, and whether you work part-time or full-time, in or outside the home, all of us need to learn to adjust to our friends' changing life circumstances. Here are four suggestions for making and keeping friends in *all* seasons of life:

1. Assess your changing friendship needs. When Meg was a manager with a large corporation, most of her friends were clients or coworkers. After she had children and decided to stay home, she was cut off from her social network. She missed the intellectual stimulation, so she sought out other women with similar interests and started a discussion group.

When faced with a new situation, ask yourself, What needs aren't being met in my current circumstances? What resources are available to meet those needs? and What can I do to take advantage of those resources?

2. Find the friendship links in your current situation. Anne became best friends with Terry while they were co-leading their daughters' Girl Scout troop. Both busy moms with little time to spare for leisurely conversations, they've managed to develop a bond while planning camping trips and service projects for a gaggle of giggly girls.

If you're feeling lonely, sit down and think through your potential friendship links. You may be surprised!

3. Enjoy the friendship benefits of each season of life. When she was single, Susan used to love going out shopping with girlfriends on Saturday afternoons. Now she has four children and can't believe she could ever do that! One consolation of her changed status, however, is a network of other young mothers who get together regularly to share their joys and struggles.

Each life season has its own potential friendship benefits. Learn to embrace them.

4. Don't be afraid to take the initiative. Karen, whose husband has been transferred several times in recent years, has learned to put the word out that she's looking for friends whenever she finds herself in a new community. After one move, for example, she contacted a women's Bible study. The very next day a woman from the group dropped by to visit and eventually became a good friend. If you're feeling a friend deficit, offer someone else the gift of your friendship—and you may find a friend!

ARE YOU AN ENCOURAGER? THE ROLE OF ENCOURAGEMENT
is vital in our world today. With so many people struggling with
job loss, relationship loss, and loss of self-esteem, now more
than ever may be the time when *you* can be the one to help a
friend face her present and future with boldness. When you
want to bolster a friend's spirits and don't know what to say, try
out these ten tips to help bring new perspective to a friend's life:

MAKE A FRIEND'S DAY BY WHAT YOU SAY
CATHERINE E. ROLLINS

GROWTH CHART Call attention to your friend's growth in a
relationship, as a person, or in her career. If you've seen
behavior or physical attributes change, tell her. "Three months
ago, you weighed fifteen pounds more than you do now!
You're doing great at that diet!" Encourage her in the establish-
ment of new habits and skills: "You had never turned on a
computer until two months ago. Look at you now!"

PUT A POSITIVE SLANT ON THE FUTURE Encourage your friend
to write down a few goals for future reference. Focusing on
a brighter tomorrow helps a person get past a gloomy
today.

POINT OUT OPTIONS With your friend's help, identify as
many options for her situation as possible. Don't dismiss
anything as being too absurd. Off-the-wall ideas frequently
trigger truly creative options. Once you've listed your options,
evaluate each one and then decide on "Plan A." Help your
friend figure out how to implement her chosen option.

KUDOS TO YOU Find something you can applaud
genuinely in your friend and be generous in doing so:
"You had me in stitches!" "I was delighted to hear your
ideas!" Tell a coworker you appreciate a well-made
presentation; let a roommate know you appreciate a meal

she prepared. Compliment your friend's appearance, choices, suggestions, or efforts.

🔅 FORGIVE Guilt weighs heavily on the soul. Three of the most encouraging words you can offer a friend are "I forgive you." Forgiveness frees. It restores. It heals. If your friend is bemoaning her failures, mistakes, or sins, say, "I don't hold this against you," or "Ask forgiveness of the one you've wronged; then forgive yourself. Move forward in your life and leave this behind you."

🔅 UP-FRONT ADMIRER Point out your friend's strengths, including natural talents and interests and personality traits you find compelling and attractive.

🔅 PASS ALONG A SMILE Pass along uplifting words: a verse of Scripture, the message on a bumper sticker, a light-hearted story in a newspaper. Let your friend know you were thinking of her and her interests, work, or projects.

🔅 NEVER SAY NEVER A friend who is stressed or burned out by the hectic pace she keeps may well be encouraged by your saying, "It's never too late to make a change."

🔅 YOU'RE NOT ALONE Encourage your friend to find a support group of people who have faced a similar situation. Also, remind her that you're choosing to "walk through the emotions" with her.

🔅 ONE OF A KIND No other person can duplicate your friend's birth, childhood, circumstances, talents, insights, opportunities, and skills. Point out the ways your friend is truly "one of a kind." Highlight the fact that she has a unique purpose in life before God. Encourage her by saying, "There has never been and there never will be another person just like you. I count it a great privilege to know you!"

WE ALL FEEL SELF-CONSCIOUS AT TIMES OR WONDER WHAT others think of us. But shy women endure these embarrassments daily. They talk to their children's teachers and their hands shake. They think about calling a troubled person but then chicken out.

If you're shy but you long to make a friend, here's how to overcome a timid spirit and risk stepping out.

Risk Stepping Out

JAN JOHNSON

I recognized Judy's car in the Safeway parking lot. As I shopped, I peeked around the corner of the aisle so she couldn't catch me unaware. There she was—squeezing the lettuce. Then out of the corner of my eye I saw her head for the checkout stand. At last I was safe. I was relieved I didn't have to talk to her. Making conversation with others was agony for me; I never knew what to say.

But when I discovered from psychologist Philip Zimbardo that shyness encourages a self-conscious preoccupation—a fixation that fosters depression, anxiety, loneliness and erects substantial roadblocks to the woman who wants to grow in God's love—I finally decided that God couldn't be pleased with my sneaking around in grocery stores to avoid talking to other people. To show God's love to others, my shyness had to go.

But could I change? Paul thought Timothy could: "For God did not give us a spirit of timidity, but a spirit of power, of love and of self-discipline" (2 Tim. 1:6-7). I longed for that. If you do, too, ask yourself these questions:

1. Am I shy or just introverted? Shy individuals fear people, certain situations, and their own inadequacies, while introverts simply prefer to be alone.

2. What situations or types of people make me shy? Although I can hold my own in most groups now, I still clam up around overbearing, gregarious people. So when I know I'll be around such persons, I think of conversational topics ahead of time.

3. What experiences have made me shy? Shyness is often related to low self-esteem. We think we have nothing important to contribute, compared to everyone else who seems so talented and capable. Instead of nursing the foggy notion that I was awkward and unattractive, I identified specific personal pluses and minuses. Sure, my figure was not picture perfect—but my complexion glowed.

To reinforce my positive qualities, I started a file folder of awards, thank-you notes, and letters of appreciation to remind me that God was able to use me. As a counterbalance, I listed my negative qualities on my daily prayer list.

4. How much do I care for others? One night as I sat silently at a party, I felt sorry for the quiet woman next to me. I opened up to try to make her feel better. I felt so good about helping her that I later tried to draw others out, seeing myself as the "shy person's rescue squad."

With my newfound confidence, I've developed a list of ritual questions about jobs, family members, and hobbies I now use in social situations. I also add "feeling" questions: "Do you like living in a condominium?" and information questions: "What does an interior designer do?" When I get stuck, I rephrase people's words: "So you think that . . ."

For Christian women, stepping out of shyness can be a spiritual journey. God stretches our faith as we rely on his love and claim his promise "Perfect love drives out fear" (1 John 4:18). As we overcome shyness, we gain confidence to tackle other problems in life.

And if you're like me, it makes it easier to go grocery shopping, too.

WHEN MY FRIEND DANA HAD HER THIRD MISCARRIAGE FOUR years ago, she grieved—and I felt helpless. The things I could do—taking her a casserole, praying for her, cleaning her house—just didn't seem enough. I wanted to do more, but what?

If your friend has recently lost a child, spouse, parent, or other loved one, you may be feeling helpless, too. You want to assist your friend, but you're not sure what to say or what to do. At such a time, your friend needs you more than ever, so don't back off from her grief. Instead, use these tips from Vicki Huffman, a woman who has grieved deeply, to show your support.

BE THERE IN THE TOUGH TIMES
VICKI HUFFMAN

After losing both my parents and my husband's parents, I've observed how friends help or inadvertently hurt those who grieve. The apostle Paul urged us to pass on the comfort we've received from the God of all comfort to others (2 Cor. 1:4). But, since death causes most of us to feel totally inept, how can we help? Here are a few ways:

💡 LET THE TEARS FLOW Hearing tears choke the voice of my friend Connie, who prayed with me on the phone as I poured out my heart during my grieving process, dislodged my own habitually stifled tears. Connie knew trying to be stoic for someone else isn't always advisable—or biblical. The apostle Paul tells us in Romans 12:15 to "mourn with those who mourn." Even Jesus wept (John 11:35) at the grave of Lazarus before raising him from the dead. So if you feel like crying for your friend, cry.

Comforting a friend may not mean drying her tears but giving her the freedom to let her tears flow, too. Those who choke back their tears may grieve more intensely later—as I did.

COMFORT WITH YOUR PRESENCE RATHER THAN YOUR WORDS
Don't feel impelled to give theological reasons for your
friend's loss. Those who help us most in our grieving don't
quote large sections of Scripture, say they know exactly
how we feel (how could they?), tell us about others in
worse situations, or assure us we'll feel better soon.
Instead, they do what a few sensitive people did for me:
They hugged me gently and said, "I'm sorry for your loss,"
"I'm praying for you," or "I love you." Sometimes they just
put their arms around me and said nothing. I learned then
how silence can be golden.

 READ CHRISTIAN BOOKS ABOUT THE GRIEVING PROCESS Even
if you haven't lost anyone close to you yet, reading books
written by those who have will help you know how to pray
for and respond to your friend who may be on an
emotional roller coaster.

 DON'T SAY, "CALL ME IF I CAN DO ANYTHING." Volunteer
by deeds instead of words. Phone your friend at least once
a week. Schedule times to visit her or go to lunch. Invite
her to social events. Send cards on special holidays she
shared with the deceased and the anniversary—monthly or
yearly—of her loss. She'll be grateful you remembered.

 TALK WITH YOUR FRIEND ABOUT HER LOVED ONE When your
friend can speak freely about her loved one and others do
as well, it helps her to know that that person won't be
forgotten. It also can be comforting to bring up your own
pleasant memories of the deceased.

 BE THERE CONSISTENTLY Grief follows no timetable. Even
years after my mother's and father's deaths, I still have
difficult moments during the Thanksgiving holiday since
they both died within a day of it. At those times I talk it out
with an understanding person. With God's help, you can
be that person for your friend.

ARE YOU LONGING FOR A FRIEND? THEN TAKE A GOOD
look at the people you "bump into" every day. Maybe it's time to
befriend your new neighbor, ask a coworker out to lunch, offer to
help a busy mom, or get involved with an intergenerational Bible
study at your church. Don't let age, marital status, or other
differences deprive you of a great friendship. Here's how to look
for unexpected friends—and find them!

Look for the Unexpected

CAMERIN J. COURTNEY

Three years ago nearly all my friends resembled me,
twentysomething, never married, career minded, childless.
Yet, when I moved from my Iowa college town to Chicago
for my first job, this changed dramatically. Suddenly I was
dining out with mothers of toddlers, going to antique fairs
with women in their forties, and attending aerobics classes
with stay-at-home moms. It was great but strange.

To be honest, women who wield diaper bags intimidated
me. They knew this whole other lingo (Nuks and sippy cups)
and lived by a completely different schedule (4:00 A.M.
feedings!). And I'd just assumed women who were old
enough to have birthed me wouldn't want to hang out with
me. But I was wrong. And as women of other ages and stages
in life got to know me, they revealed similar fears: Would a
young single woman find a mom of teens interesting? I
would, and I do. When we all got past our fears and reservations, some great friendships developed.

Although people from other walks of life may be less
convenient to get to know and even a bit intimidating, I've
learned they make wonderful friends. Whether you're in
your twenties or forties, married, single, or single again,
child-free, a mother, or a grandmother, here's why it's

worth pursuing friendships with women outside your comfort zone.

THEY KNOW STUFF YOU DON'T

One of the first people I got to know at my new job was Jan.
She was a single, forty-year-old woman
who worked in the office next to mine. I
learned she was into gardening, interior
design, and *Color Me Beautiful*. And,
more important, she was willing to share
all this information with me, her twenty-
two-year-old coworker.

Within months Jan had me pegged as an
"autumn" and told me which colors looked
best on me in my slowly expanding work
wardrobe. A year later she helped me move
into a new apartment and even stayed around
to help arrange the furniture and decorations.

THEY HELP DISPEL STEREOTYPES

The evening news, movies, and magazines would have us believe all Genera-
tion Xers are whiny slackers who are
short on personal hygiene and long on
contempt for the world. I've met more
than one woman who's bought into this
stereotype and expressed surprise when
she discovered I'm a normal, function-
ing human being who falls into this age
bracket.

*As a single woman, for
many years I hoped
my frantic social activ-
ity would meet my
need to be loved, and
I got involved in some
bad relationships. But
as I've moved into my
thirties, I've learned a
lot about balance.
At my birthday party
last year, I was over-
whelmed with grati-
tude for the close
friendships God
brought into my life
when I let go of the
unhealthy ones.*

KATHY TROCCOLI

As frustrated as the Gen-X stereotype makes me, I must
admit I've bought into a few stereotypes of my own. For
example, I used to think when you grow older, you slow
down and life becomes a bit boring. That was until I met
Gloria, a sixty-three-year-old woman in the exercise class I
lead. She's one of my most dedicated students. And when she

does miss a class, it's usually because she's learning about painting, pottery making, bread baking, or ballroom dancing in a class somewhere else.

And there's Barb, my fiftysomething coworker who, along with her sixtysomething husband, is constantly flying overseas for vacations in places like the Holy Land and Bermuda.

These women are more than sterotype-defying models of older age; they're my friends. And through our conversations I've learned older women have a lot more spunk than I've ever given them credit for.

THEY OFFER JOY FROM THE PAST AND HOPE FOR THE FUTURE

I'm one of two single women on my immediate staff of eighteen people. Consequently, whenever I mention a man's name or talk about an outing that remotely resembles a date, I'm met with many raised eyebrows from my female friends in the office. When I receive flowers, I don't know who's more excited, my married coworkers or me.

"We're just reliving our single years through you, you know," Louise, a thirty-four-year-old coworker, told me one day after I'd answered a barrage of questions from her and several others about a special date. I know, and I kind of enjoy it. Letting my married friends vicariously enjoy the best of being single is the least I can do to show my appreciation for their relationship advice. And besides, that's what friends are for!

On the flip side, being around so many married friends gives me a clear-cut vision of how great marriage can be. It gives me a renewed hope that sometimes dreams do come true and it really is worth the wait for God's perfect timing.

THEY REMIND YOU THAT THE GRASS IS PRETTY GREEN ON YOUR SIDE OF THE FENCE, TOO

A few weeks ago on a Saturday morning, Louise and I, united by our common love of cheesecake, went on a mission: to find, to buy, to indulge. Louise's two sons—Scott, eight, and Alex, two—went with us. I'd almost forgotten how much fun being around kids can be. As Scott told me about what he was learning in school and Alex played peekaboo with me, I could hear my biological clock ticking louder and louder.

Give others a chance—
you never know what
they will become!

HEATHER WHITESTONE

But as the morning wore on, I was also reminded of how much work little ones can be. When we got out of the car to go into the stores, we had to locate mittens and boots that had been flung into the back of the minivan in an act of two-year-old defiance. We lugged out the stroller . . . and a blanket . . . and a favorite toy. As I watched Louise mediate sibling warfare, the ticking got fainter and fainter.

Later that afternoon, when I ran a few errands by myself, I noticed the ease with which I whizzed in and out of the car. The only thing I had to lug around was my purse. And there in the middle of the grocery store parking lot, I silently thanked God for this child-free time in my life. Perhaps someday I'll enjoy the special title "Mommy" and all the blessings that go along with it—but for now I need to appreciate the blessings of freedom and ease.

When I think back over the past three years, I realize how much I would have missed if I'd allowed myself to remain paralyzed by the mistaken notion that young mothers don't have time for friends or that older women have nothing to gain from friendship with someone half their age. God's blessings come in all shapes and sizes. Once we discover that, reaching out to people of different ages or stages in life becomes an adventure. Stepping outside my comfort zone has never been more rewarding.

SOME THINGS ARE UNFORGETTABLE: THE TIME YOU HAD the flu and a friend brought you homemade chicken soup; the night your boyfriend asked you to marry him and your roommate got out of bed to celebrate with you; the day a friend was diagnosed with cancer and you booked a flight so you could pray and cry with her.

Friends are necessary to our health and well-being. They are God's timely gifts to us. As the seasons of life change, they meet our needs and we meet theirs. Where is the gift of your friendship needed today? That's what this next story is about.

Meet a Need

MAYO MATHERS

"What's the best present you've ever received?" someone asked me recently. It only took me a few moments to respond. My favorite gift, though delivered by a neighbor, came straight from God at a time when I was grieving the loss of a family friend.

Ralph was a forty-four-year-old father of five. We'd invested fifteen years into weaving our two families together into a sturdy fabric of friendship. While he and his family were moving into a new home, Ralph suddenly died of a heart attack, catapulting us into a state of profound shock.

Our family quickly gathered up Ralph's wife, Sandee, and their children and brought them to our home. Through the numbness we helped Sandee face the endless details surrounding her husband's death.

Meanwhile, our house bulged with people as their friends and out-of-town relatives arrived for the funeral. We set up camping trailers in our driveway and rolled out sleeping bags in the house. Caring for everyone was a welcome distraction, yet my increasing weariness made it more and more difficult.

The morning of the funeral, I woke up to find Ralph's

elderly father standing over me. "Eh! Eh!" he said, pointing toward the kitchen. A recent stroke had robbed him of the ability to communicate, but I understood he wanted breakfast.

Every muscle in my body screamed as I struggled to my feet. Even the simple task of perking coffee seemed a gigantic chore. *How can I possibly manage to feed the nearly thirty people asleep under my roof?* I groaned inwardly. A balloon of panic inflated inside me, threatening to burst.

Oh, God . . . I was too weary to even finish the prayer as I looked around my kitchen. Every inch of counter space was stacked with the cakes, pies, and bags of chips friends had been bringing for four days. My refrigerator brimmed with casseroles and salads. I could feed the whole town with this food—but none of it was suitable for breakfast.

The phone rang, and I lunged for the distraction it offered.

"What's for breakfast?" chirped the cheerful voice on the other end.

Another person to feed! I thought in despair. As I stammered, the voice I now recognized as my neighbor's interrupted. "Don't fix a thing. I just took two pans of homemade cinnamon rolls out of the oven. I thought you might need them."

A few minutes later my house was filled with the savory odor of cinnamon rolls—enough for everyone. I scooped one out and bit into its buttery warmth. *God saw my floundering and met my need through a friend!*

Since that morning the spicy aroma of cinnamon rolls always reminds me of God's timely gift. For that reason, I want to continue to fill others' houses with the spicy aroma of God's love. It's a gift worth repeating.

THINK IT OVER

What season of friendship are you in? Are you lonely, wishing you had a closer friend? Are you looking for friends who can understand more where you are in life right now? Do you have extra time you could give someone who's hurting?

Whatever your season, ask God to open your heart and your world to unexpected friends. Then look for his surprises!

Health and Fitness

Last year the discovery of a lump in my breast sent me
running to my doctor in panic. I had always taken
my health for granted—but suddenly not anymore.
The good news is, I was fine. But I've learned that while
the ultimate state of my physical well-being belongs in
God's hands, there are lots of ways I can safeguard
this precious gift of health. I need to be vigilant,
whether it's making sure I get my annual physical,
watching what I eat, or trying to incorporate
some exercise into my very hectic lifestyle.

JANE JOHNSON STRUCK

How's Your Health?

DO you have the sniffles? a few extra pounds? Are you feeling discouraged, even depressed? Your health—physical, emotional, mental, and spiritual well-being—is an extremely important part of your life. Good health can lift your spirits, boost your energy, relieve aches and pains, and give you a new perspective. Someone once said, "If you've got your health, you've got everything." It's not always easy to schedule in that doctor's visit, change that eating habit, call a counselor, or begin an exercise program. But it's well worth the effort—not only for yourself but for those you love.

All of us have some health habit (or nonhabit) that we could improve. Maybe you hate exercise or eat more than you need. Maybe you hold anger inside from a past event. But in order to have the balanced life God calls us to, we need to be healthy—in *all* ways. And that's what this chapter is about.

MOST OF THE YEAR I FEEL REASONABLY FIT. KNOWN FOR full-speed dashes down office hallways, I work off a lot of calories. But with staff who teach aerobics, swim, work out at the club, walk during lunch, and use the treadmill at home, it's hard not to feel guilty.

The truth is, I'd rather do *anything* but exercise. Because the very word suggests bodily torture (they don't call it *working out* for nothing), I've placated my guilt the last two years with the I'm-too-busy-to-exercise excuse.

But no more. I've discovered that exercise can be fun—and inspirational. Here's how.

Walk Your Way to Fitness

HOLLY G. MILLER

Spring arrived—and I was feeling flabby and fatigued. "You need to exercise," my husband, the jogger, prescribed. He reminded me May 1 was a couple of weeks away (I have a habit of announcing diets and other good intentions on the first of every month) and challenged me to pick and stick with a fitness program.

But *what* program? I refused to rearrange furniture for daily workouts with a celebrity on tape, and I wasn't willing to trade in the family car on a pricey living-room ski machine. I ruled out seasonal activities and turned thumbs down on anything involving cumbersome gear (skis, rackets, golf clubs) or a special setting (pool, court, or rink). It couldn't be expensive, and, since I travel a lot, it had to be portable. What could I enjoy doing regardless of my age (forget the rollerblades!) and the availability of a second person?

Only one shape-up plan met my criteria. A few days before my May 1 deadline, I announced my decision: I would *walk* my way to fitness.

I mapped out a four-mile loop around my neighborhood

and vowed to follow the circuit daily until the first of August. On that date I would review the strides I'd made and decide if exercise really improved the way I looked and felt. Se-

cretly, I hoped my plan would go the way of the trampoline that had been the hit of my last garage sale. Then I could mutter a few "I told you so's" to my husband and revert to my couch-potato ways.

Changes came subtly. Yet within a month, my energy went up, my weight came down, and my spiritual life improved. I stepped away from distractions, turned my mind to the Lord, listened to inspirational music, and "read" good books as I simultaneously tallied my miles.

By August, friends noticed the differences I'd felt for months. "What's your secret?" they prodded. "New health club? A fitness trainer?" My explanation seemed too simple to believe. I challenged them to try it, and I offered eight pieces of step-by-step advice:

Women who work out develop not only a better outlook but also a faster metabolism, burning fat more efficiently. And you'll reap the benefits of taking care of the body God gave you—improved physical, emotional, and spiritual health!

LINDA PIEPENBRINK

1. Assemble your gear. Every serious walker should invest in comfortable shoes (break them in slowly), an umbrella that fits into your jacket pocket, and a radio/tape recorder with earphones. I've never been tempted to buy designer warm-ups or expensive superstar-endorsed footwear. My only splurge has been an oversized sweatshirt with the bumper-sticker message: "Walkers Take It All in Stride."

2. Plot your course. Select three different routes that will provide variety and flexibility. You'll need a short route (a mile and a half) for busy days when you can spare only twenty minutes. Two longer routes (two miles and four miles) are suitable for more leisurely days. I try to follow the longest route at least three times a week. Sometimes I set off on a short walk, then change plans midway as my energy builds and my stress diminishes.

3. Have a rain plan. Malls are no substitute for the great outdoors, but in a downpour mall walking is a way to stay true to your exercise plan without risking the sniffles.

4. Commit to a three-month schedule. Results may come slowly, so make a pact with yourself not to pass judgment on your program until you've given it a ninety-day trial. In the beginning, try to walk at the same hour until exercise becomes a part of your routine. After that, depending on your job, family, and the season, you can adjust the time of day and length of your walk.

5. Design a program. To prevent walks from becoming ho-hum—the most scenic landscape loses its allure after a few weeks—build a program that exercises your mind and spirit as well as your body. The two complaints I hear most often from Christian women are: "I'm too busy to exercise" and "I know I should spend regular time with the Lord, but there aren't enough hours in the day." My answer: Combine the two.

Some days I put on my "ears" and tune my portable radio to the local Christian radio station for inspirational music or a good talk show. Other days I listen to the Bible on tape, a motivational speaker, or a best-selling book read by its Christian author. Sometimes I read Scripture before I leave home and carry a verse with me to mull over or memorize.

6. Fortify yourself. I always indulge in a light snack before I walk. This prevents gnawing hunger pains or—worse yet—dizziness from distracting me. A piece of fruit or a small bowl of cereal is enough to appease a grumbling tummy. After the walk, a large glass of water replenishes the liquid lost through perspiration.

7. Pick up the pace. One of the advantages of walking is it isn't competitive. However, I like to time my walks and gradually shave off seconds as I improve my speed. Because I walk at a comfortable but brisk clip, I always do a few stretching exercises before I leave home and when I return. These help to loosen muscles and reduce stiffness.

8. Invite a friend. For variety, I sometimes ask a friend or my spouse to tag along. Wonderful conversations occur when the phone doesn't ring, kids don't dash in and out, and we're miles from the closest television! My husband, the jogger, sometimes joins me on Friday evenings. Our dialogue begins with a rehash of the week's highs and lows and ends with plans for the weekend. Over the course of four miles, we shed the stress of our jobs and slip into our off-duty mode. By the time we arrive back at our doorstep, we've made the transition from work to weekend and are ready to relax.

Physical fitness isn't my life—it's part of my life. When God becomes your first priority, fitness can be one of the pieces that helps you feel good about who you are. But it shouldn't be your first priority. You can look good even if you have short legs or a thick waist. You don't have to look like a model in a magazine.

KATHY TROCCOLI

After two years as a determined trekker, my progress report reads something like this: I've tallied more than two thousand miles, consumed more than a hundred library books on tape, dropped several pounds, and lost a few inches. More important, my spiritual life has been enriched as I've walked away from the pressures of house and family and concentrated on my walk with the Lord. Problems diminish and solutions surface when I'm nudged outside and into God's world. I work my way through difficult situations one step at a time and, when faced with a really tough decision, feel no need to "sleep on it." Instead, I walk it out!

WHETHER YOU AVOID THE DOCTOR'S OFFICE LIKE THE plague or visit often enough to earn your own parking space, it's important to remember the best health care is rarely obtained by chance. So if you're moving to a new community, switching insurance plans, or dissatisfied with your current health-care provider and are thinking about making a change, here are some guidelines to help you find a doctor you're comfortable with—and to make that doctor visit more productive.

Make the Most of Your Doctor Visit

DR. PAUL REISSER

If you're looking to select a doctor, consider the following:

1. Decide what type of medical office you prefer as "home base." Even if you have a complex medical history, it's wise to have a primary-care physician who knows your "whole story" and can deal with day-to-day problems.

2. Ask around. Take an informal poll in your church, neighborhood, or workplace to see which doctors or clinics are mentioned most often. Women with pro-life convictions usually prefer to see gynecologists who don't perform abortions (local crisis pregnancy centers or other pro-life organizations usually maintain a list of abortionists).

3. Consider a "get acquainted" session. If you've narrowed your list but aren't sure of your choice, set up a meet-the-doctor visit and

- see how you're treated on the phone. Does the person at the other end of the line sound friendly and pleasant or harried and hostile?
- check out the office. Do you feel welcome? Does it feel like a place that will help you stay calm in a crisis?

■ briefly talk with the doctor. If you have lots of questions about the practice, someone on the office staff may be able to answer them for you.

Once you've picked the practice, here's how to get the most out of your contacts with the doctor and office staff.

1. Let the appointment person know what you need to talk about. The time allotted may depend on the number and types of concerns you have.

2. Don't insist you'll "speak only to the doctor and no one else." This usually delays getting your problem solved. Nearly every doctor relies heavily on a nurse to screen medical calls.

3. Let the doctor know what's on your agenda. If you have more than one item to talk about, make a list and give it to the caregiver at the beginning of your visit.

4. Don't bring a surprise guest (i.e., "While we're here, would you look in Jennie's ear?").

5. Make friends with the office staff. If you're particularly friendly, cooperative, and even complimentary, you'll make their day—and probably get better service.

6. Don't push the wrong friendship buttons. If you know the doctor outside the office setting, don't try to use this to bypass normal office procedures.

7. Respect your doctor's off-duty boundaries. The supermarket, mall, and especially the church aren't extensions of his or her office.

8. Don't be afraid to ask questions. It's always appropriate to understand what your doctor recommends and what the risks and benefits of any proposed treatment are.

IF YOUR (OR YOUR FAMILY'S) "IMMUNE IQ" CURRENTLY ISN'T very high, don't just accept coughs, colds, the flu, etc. as a normal course of events in your family. Many small actions can pay off big dividends in increased resistance to disease. Here are ten simple tips for staying healthier—and happier!

INCREASE YOUR IMMUNE IQ
VICTORIA WILDS FULLER

💡 NAIL BITERS ANONYMOUS Most viruses spread by our hands enter the body through the mouth or nose. Wash and dry your hands often (soap isn't necessary) and keep hands away from your face. Change hand towels daily, and use a germ-killing cleaner on frequently touched surfaces (such as refrigerator handle and telephone). And stop biting those nails!

💡 TAKE A WALK Regular exercise actually increases the number of "T" cells (germ fighters in our bloodstream). Stress tends to suppress formation of white blood cells (disease fighters), but exercise relieves stress. Sunlight triggers our body's natural energy boosters to banish depression, so you will be less likely to overeat or fight with your family. The next time you're tempted to watch TV, get out of that chair—and take a walk instead.

💡 VEGGIES AND FRUIT ARE GOOD FOR YOU Eat a carrot and an orange. Both vitamins A and C are crucial to the immune system. Additionally, carrots and oranges both give a natural rise in blood glucose level without the detrimental effects of refined sugar. As with other low-fat, high-fiber foods, they also may protect against some forms of cancer. So eat up those orange foods, and enjoy. They're good—and good for you!

💡 DEAL CONSTRUCTIVELY WITH ANGER Some studies suggest that anger—even if it's repressed—burns up large amounts of the body's disease-fighting vitamin C. If you're struggling with resentment or anger, talk it out with a spouse, friend, or counselor *before* it takes over your physical, emotional, and mental health. The healthy people are those who know when to ask for help.

💡 CLEAN YOUR TOOTHBRUSH The moist environment of toothbrush holders makes an ideal habitat for germs. Especially if your family has recurrent sore throats or colds, carefully clean toothbrushes and holder weekly. A soak in hydrogen peroxide or a cycle through the dishwasher are two easy ways to kill the germs.

💡 CALL A FRIEND Supportive relationships actually seem to lead to increased levels of "T" cell disease fighters in our bloodstream. So the next time you feel down, call a friend, and have a good chat—or arrange your next get-together.

💡 LAUGH! Whether your taste runs to *I Love Lucy* reruns or "Far Side" cartoons, a hearty chuckle relieves pain and tension, enhances circulation, aids digestion, and lowers blood pressure. Laughter *is* good medicine, so laugh it up!

💡 STUDY GOD'S WORD DAILY Researchers have identified certain thought patterns that seem to contribute to major diseases. Hopelessness and helplessness are two. Regular Bible study helps us live out our life empowered by faith.

💡 THINK UP The Bible calls us to think on pure and praise-worthy things (see Phil. 4:8). Research implies that habitual exposure to violent, terrifying, or depressing movies, TV, music, or books can negatively affect our immune system. So think positively, and choose positive entertainment. It'll make a difference in your overall health.

FAST-FOOD MEALS EATEN BEHIND THE WHEEL—SOUND familiar? In our hectic lives, eating to fill all our nutritional requirements, while meeting our time requirements, can be a real challenge. However, careful convenience food selections (whether fast or frozen) can yield a diet that is nutritious *and* quick! If you want to be smart about fast food, follow these easy suggestions.

Get Smart about Fast Food

DRS. SHARON AND DAVID SNEED

Although none of our fast-food choices are the best examples of vitamin-packed, nutritious meals, we now have more acceptable options than ever before. To make the right fast-food choices, keep these factors in mind:

1. Hold the mayo! Avoid ordering selections with mayonnaise, tartar sauce, "special sauces," or any other creamy dressing. Instead, learn to love mustard. It even tastes great on grilled chicken sandwiches. Catsup is also fine, though it contains one-third sugar. Adding mayo to a large hamburger adds 150 calories of pure fat.

2. Just say no to fried. A plain onion is a mere 25 calories. If you turn it into onion rings, it can approach 400 calories or more, depending on the recipe.

3. Salads are usually a good choice. One major flaw in the nutritional value of fast foods is they are frequently low in the vitamins and minerals supplied by fresh fruits and vegetables. If you eat from a salad bar, however, items such as fresh spinach, tomatoes, bell peppers, carrots, and fruits can supply these nutrients. The greener the leaves, the greater the vitamin content, so try fresh spinach as a salad base instead of lettuce for a vitamin-packed meal.

4. Salad dressings? Carry your own. Most regular salad dressings are between 60 and 90 calories per tablespoon. If you add four tablespoons to the top of your salad, you have just added the caloric equivalent of a hamburger. Actually, a hamburger would make a better choice; salad dressings are pure fat, while a burger is only 30 to 40 percent fat. If you want to order a salad and use a salad dressing, bring your own—or ask for a "lite" alternative of 25 calories per tablespoon or less.

5. Stay away from creamy salads, such as tuna, chicken, or potato salad, that can be laden with heavy mayonnaise. Mashed potatoes and gravy can have half the calories of cole slaw. Never turn down a lean ham or roast beef sandwich with mustard in lieu of a tuna or chicken salad sandwich. The former will have much less fat and fewer calories.

6. Avoid sugary beverages. Instead, try iced tea or water with lemon, a sugar-free soda, or black coffee. Remember that most nondairy creamers are just as fatty as real cream but contain tropical oils instead of butterfat.

7. Never say cheese, please, if you are trying to control calories, cholesterol, or fat intake. Regular cheese, often touted as a health food, is actually 80 percent fat. This makes it a generally poor food choice for everyone except children.

8. Don't repeat the same mistakes. Avoid places that will lead you astray with fast-food choices. If there is a particular food item you find so tempting you can't resist, get out of the habit of going where it's served. Within a few months, that particular food item may no longer be appealing.

IF YOUR SCHEDULE IS IN FULL, FRANTIC SWING, IT'S EASY TO feel a bit down. When we asked TCW readers what they do when they get the blues, we were besieged with a flurry of creative pick-me-ups. They're sure to bring the joy back to your life, no matter how busy you are, and give you some brainstorms of your own.

FIND WAYS TO BEAT THE BLUES

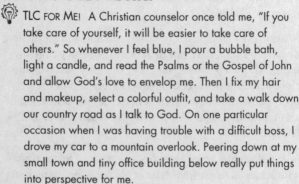

 TLC FOR ME! A Christian counselor once told me, "If you take care of yourself, it will be easier to take care of others." So whenever I feel blue, I pour a bubble bath, light a candle, and read the Psalms or the Gospel of John and allow God's love to envelop me. Then I fix my hair and makeup, select a colorful outfit, and take a walk down our country road as I talk to God. On one particular occasion when I was having trouble with a difficult boss, I drove my car to a mountain overlook. Peering down at my small town and tiny office building below really put things into perspective for me.

SARA RAPP

CLEAN SWEEP Sometimes when I'm feeling blue, it's because my apartment is messy. So I turn up the lights, put on some upbeat music, and for about fifteen minutes do a quick sweep through each room—emptying trash baskets, washing the dishes, making my bed, and putting away clutter. Then I'll light several vanilla-scented candles, curl up with a good book under a cozy afghan, and enjoy my now-clean apartment.

CINDY LEARNED

 TUNE UP I have a set of instrumental praise hymns on CDs that always kick a sad mood. I inevitably begin singing along—even though my singing leaves much to be

desired! When I'm caught up in praising God, I forget
whatever has made me sad.

ALANE PEARCE

 FUTURE FUN When I find myself getting depressed, I give
myself something to look forward to—a long bath after I
get all the children in bed or a phone call to my mother or
a friend to plan a get-together. Somehow knowing I have
something nice to look forward to helps me take the focus
off my blue mood.

KAREN R. GOOD

 CHOCOLATE THERAPY Sometimes there's just no way around
it—curling up in a comfy chair with a scoop of chocolate
ice cream improves my disposition greatly!

CAROL ANN MCGIFFIN

 A LAUGH A DAY Laughter is one of my favorite ways to
beat the blues. In college, a friend and I created a book
called *Our Funniest and Most Embarrassing College
Moments.* Looking through that book now reminds me of
the times we accidentally dyed our hair purple, wrote
notes to each other in class, threw Frisbees in the rain—
and always gives me a good chuckle! As Proverbs 17:22
says, "A cheerful heart is good medicine."

SHARON EVANS

 BOX-O-BLESSINGS In my room I keep a box on which is
written: "Thank you, Lord, for . . ." Every time God sends a
new blessing into my life, I write it on a slip of paper and
put it in. When I feel he's deserted me, I need only to look
in that box to find evidence of his faithfulness!

SUZANNE EMRY

"BEAUTY IS MORE THAN SKIN-DEEP," MY MOTHER WOULD always tell me during my skinny, underdeveloped adolescent years. "God cares about your heart. Make sure you're beautiful inside, where it counts." Although I believed her, I still wished for the dark hair, olive skin, and perfect figure of my friend Marianne.

Today there are still times (fewer now, thank goodness) when I wish I looked like someone else. And based on all the letters I receive from women, I know I'm not the only one. Meet Renate Shafter, a woman who struggled with her body—and gradually learned to love it.

Learn to Love Your Body

RENATE SHAFTER

I was eleven when I first felt dissatisfied with my body. I had a best friend named Lynnie, whose Jordache jeans fit her Barbie-doll hips with svelte perfection. Although our heights and weights were similar, Lynnie's body resembled a slender rectangle, mine was pearlike. My curving thighs and rounded behind seemed out of proportion when contrasted with Lynnie's straight lines. I came to the obvious conclusion—I was wearing the wrong brand of jeans.

I dragged my mom to the store and tried on a pair of Jordache jeans. To my dismay, the same curves stared back at me from all the wrong places. In a panic, I tried on pair after pair of jeans. Each time I looked nothing like Lynnie. I left the store in a brooding, jeanless silence. *The problem isn't with my jeans,* I realized. *It's with my body!*

At home I rummaged through my parents' bookcase and found a book called *Thin Thighs in Thirty Days*. I read through it and began the program, which included a diet, thigh exercises, and a daily walk.

When my parents interfered with my dieting plans, I knew attaining my ideal body would have to be done in secret. I ate small, low-fat portions of breakfast and dinner and threw away the lunches Mom packed for me.

By the time I entered eighth grade, I'd reduced my five-foot-three-inch frame to ninety pounds. My body lost the fat it needed to maintain a healthy

God didn't design us to live on the run.

TWILA PARIS

reproductive cycle. When my periods stopped, my mom assumed it was simply the irregularity common to many young girls and suspected nothing. Since I was involved in gymnastics and volleyball, Mom figured I was an active, healthy teenager with a harmless tendency to diet.

One evening my parents and two younger sisters were watching television and eating ice cream. I, as usual, abstained. "Why don't you have just one small scoop?" my mom said. "It won't kill you." After wrestling with myself for a few minutes in the kitchen, I indulged in a scoop of chocolate chip ice cream . . . then another . . . until I'd eaten twelve scoops!

After that night, binges became an uncontrollable part of my life. But I planned them so no single person ever saw me eat more than a normal amount of food. After each binge subsided, I vowed to change. I'd create new rules, a new diet, praying fervently it would work this time. Then, terrified of the ten or fifteen pounds I'd gain, I'd starve myself and exercise fanatically to get skinny again.

My family and friends had no inkling of the internal war I waged. I was a straight-A student, involved in sports, dance, and choir. On the surface, I had it all. But my hated pattern persisted.

In the midst of my self-reform efforts, I decided to go to church every Sunday. I chose a nearby church, and my mom and I attended regularly. The pastor spoke about a connection to Jesus Christ that went far beyond Sunday mornings, and his words intrigued me. I started reading my Bible and praying, eager to learn more. Through gradual exploration, I became a follower of Christ. But when my prayers for healing went unanswered, I felt abandoned and confused.

By the time I finished ninth grade, I still hadn't regained a menstrual cycle. My mom took me to a doctor, who put me through a battery of tests and gave me a bottle of hormone pills but didn't ask about my eating and exercise habits.

Toward the end of tenth grade, my binges became more severe. Finally I sat down with my mom, told her about my binges, and asked for professional help. She immediately got me involved with a psychologist and an eating-disorder support group for anorexia nervosa and bulimia. Interacting with people who understood what I battled was an immense relief, but therapy didn't provide the instant solution I expected. After six months, I stopped going.

The summer before my senior year of high school, I began to date David, the man who eventually became my husband. He was a strong Christian and soon became my best friend. But it took me almost a year to tell him about my disorder. I expected him to recoil, but he was deeply saddened by my struggle. After that, he often told me how beautiful he thought I was and periodically asked me about my progress.

In college my binges lasted longer than before. My weight fluctuated wildly; I often lost or gained as much as twenty pounds in the span of a month. One spring afternoon when I was particularly despairing, David put his arm around me. "You need to accept your body the way it is," he said.

"I can't!" I cried.

Loving and accepting my body sounded impossible. My obsession with thinness was woven into my very being. But in that moment of despair, I knew that only as I loved and accepted my present self would healing come.

I clung to Luke 1:37: "For nothing is impossible with God," and abandoned dieting. I concentrated on eating when I was hungry and stopping when I was full. And every day I prayed: "Lord, renew my mind, and help me to love my body the way it is."

I also turned away from the media's narrow standard for female beauty and embraced God's all-encompassing concept of beauty. I averted my eyes when surrounded by magazine covers I knew could make me stumble and avoided television shows and movies that showcased scantily clad women. I broadened my definition of beauty by concentrating on beautiful internal traits in the women around me, including myself.

It's tough to balance concern for appearance with who we are on the inside—the part of us that lasts forever. I often ask myself, Do I spend as much time with the Lord developing my spirit as I do exercising?

KIM HILL

It didn't happen overnight, but renewing my mind daily and striving to love my body led to complete healing in my eating and exercise habits. In the past four and a half years, I haven't had a single binge or gone on any diet. I lead an active lifestyle, but I choose activities I truly enjoy, like hiking and dance classes, and do them because they give me energy—not because they might make me thin.

Sometimes I'm bombarded with irrational thoughts, and despite David's loving assurances, I wonder if he secretly wishes he married model Elle McPherson instead of me. But my good days far outnumber my bad. Despite occasional struggles I feel victorious when I see how far God has brought me.

With God's help, I can now leave grocery checkout aisles admiring the hourglass shape of the *Glamour* cover model. Yet I feel equal admiration for the healthy, beautiful pear shape I glimpse in the reflection of my car window as I put my groceries inside.

DO YOU HAVE A CASE OF "THE TIREDS"? MAYBE YOU DRAG your feet in the morning, or by midafternoon you feel like you need five cups of coffee just to stay awake. Or maybe, due to a new baby, a family crisis, or a hectic life in general, you haven't been able to get a full night's sleep for a long period of time.

If the tireds have caught up with you, this advice from Drs. Sharon and David Sneed is a must-read.

Rest When You're Tired
DRS. SHARON AND DAVID SNEED

"I feel so lethargic all the time! I wake up in the morning feeling as tired as I did when I went to bed," one of my patients, Ellen, recently complained. She—along with 12 million other Americans who visited their doctors last year troubled by symptoms of fatigue—wanted a medical explanation for the weariness that plagued her. As I talked with her about her symptoms, I learned that Ellen held down a full-time job, had two small children, cared for an ill relative, and led a women's Bible study. Her physical and emotional reserves were running on empty.

If you, like Ellen, feel tired all the time, here's what you should do:

1. Identify the source of your fatigue. Are you overcommitted? depressed? Sometimes Christians find it difficult to relax. We feel guilty if we're not busy "redeeming the time" or knocking ourselves out meeting the needs around us. But overcommitment can seriously affect your physical health, and persistent fatigue can cause physical and biological changes in your body that reduce your overall effectiveness.

But beyond overcommitment, more than half of fatigue problems can be related to anxiety, anger, chronic conflict, and depression. This doesn't mean that your fatigue is "all in your head," but that your mental state can have profound effects on your body. The stress of painful emotions is just as likely to cause fatigue as any physical disorder.

For example, symptoms of clinical depression often include fatigue, persistent sadness or irritability, disinterest in job or hobbies, unwarranted guilt, appetite changes, sleep disturbances, and sexual dysfunction. If recognized, treatment for depression with antidepressant medication and counseling can bring about rapid and effective resolution.

2. Have a medical checkup. If you wake up in the morning feeling rested but tire quickly during the day, it is more likely you have a physical problem, such as diabetes, thyroid disorder, anemia, or chronic fatigue syndrome. To uncover the cause of your fatigue, you should have a complete physical exam (including laboratory tests to evaluate each major organ of your body) to rule out physical causes. Have your doctor review any medications you might be taking, as fatigue is sometimes an unwanted side effect of prescription medications.

3. Be good to yourself. After identifying the cause of your fatigue, appropriate treatment can begin. Whatever the cause and proposed treatment, a successful regimen must include correction of poor health habits and improvement of physical conditioning. Many people take their bodies for granted for so long they forget what it's like to feel good. Elimination of unhealthy habits, proper use of medication, counseling if needed, a good diet, and a sensible exercise program will restore good health and physical vigor to the majority of those who make the effort.

THINK IT OVER
How do you feel, on a daily basis? Is it time for more exercise, healthier eating habits, a counseling visit, a doctor checkup? If so, don't wait. This week is a great time to start feeling better!

Home and Hospitality

My brothers, sisters, and I always knew God was central in our home because he was so loved and honored by both my parents. By my dad's example in the home, I knew God was great and Jesus was Lord. And Mother taught me by her example of home and hospitality that there's nothing more satisfying than a personal love relationship with the Lord. It's what made her strong.

ANNE GRAHAM LOTZ

WHAT'S YOUR HOSPITALITY IQ?

I'LL never forget the holiday I spent with strangers.

I was a college senior, en route with my sister and her husband to our parents' home in Canada, when a fierce snowstorm struck. Within minutes, our compact car, laden with luggage and gifts, slid into a ditch. After fruitless shoveling, we huddled together under blankets in the back seat—and prayed. We knew our chances of being rescued quickly in such dangerous weather were slim.

But a few hours later, there was a knock on our car roof. Our rescuer, who "just happened" to be the only tow-truck driver in that rural town, ended up taking us to his parents' farm to spend the night. They gave us pajamas, toothbrushes, and a room of our own. And on Christmas morning we awoke to find stockings filled with goodies—for us! After eating dinner with them, the weather cleared, and our rescuer towed the car to his shop and checked it over.

That afternoon as we drove off, we were teary-eyed. These people had made us feel, as the Shaker motto says, "kindly welcome." Now *that's* the kind of home and hospitality Christ calls us to. Sound impossible? It's not really. No matter what your personality is, how much time you have, or what your energy level is, this chapter will help show you how.

DO YOU ENJOY CHATTING WITH YOUR GUESTS—OR WOULD
you rather be in the kitchen, whipping up a dessert or the
dishes? Do you plan the menu in advance—or just offer your
typical Tuesday-night family fare (macaroni-and-cheese with
carrot sticks)? No matter what type of hostess we are, there's
always someone else who seems to be more organized, more
stylish, or better at the "home and hospitality" thing than we
are. But guess what? The most important part of answering
Christ's call to reach out to others is simply *being yourself*.
Here's why.

Be Yourself

SUZANNE M. GRISSOM

My husband, Jim, says I have chronic PMS. Oh . . . it's not
what you think—it's "Perpetual Martha Syndrome." And, as
my husband will attest, like Martha of Bethany—who welcomed Jesus into her home for dinner but didn't have time to
sit still and listen to him—I have a tough time sitting still. It's
just there's so much to do and the list is never-ending! But in
spite of getting a lot done, I've seen my identification with
Martha as a negative trait that needed changing.

I've heard countless sermons on the story of Martha's
dinner party (Luke 10:38-42), and basically, they've all crit-
icized Martha, the one busily preparing a meal for all her
guests, and glorified Mary, the one quietly sitting at Christ's
feet. Inevitably my response to such sermons has been a
great wave of guilt and conviction followed by a note to
myself on the fridge: "BE MARY . . . NOT MARTHA!"

For the next week or two I'd try to be Mary; I'd try to sit
quietly and listen to the Lord. But soon I'd be picking lint
fuzz balls from the couch as my mind raced ahead to my "To
Do" list. Before long, I'd go back to feeding the baby with
one hand and clipping coupons with the other. I'd catch

myself making mental memos of calls to make while bathing the dog, then making those calls on the cordless phone while pruning the roses. When baking bread, I'd put the dough in a covered bowl in the trunk of my car to rise and punch it down while out running errands.

Some of us thrill to the challenge of paring our possessions down to a box load—while others of us save empty boxes because they might come in handy some day. Somewhere between "sparse" and "stuffed" is that happy territory called livable.

JEANNE ZORNES

I remember one evening in particular when we had company. After dessert, we decided to play a board game. As each person took his or her turn, I'd run to the kitchen and do a few dishes. By the time we finished the game, the dishes were done. "Sit down, Martha," my husband chided. I did—knowing I could now enjoy our company with a clear conscience and clean dishes. The next night I folded laundry and wrote thank-you notes throughout the movie we'd rented— Martha was back!

One afternoon while I was scrubbing the kitchen floor and praying, it hit me—maybe Martha wasn't such a misdirected gal after all. Maybe she'd just gotten a bad rap. Maybe all she needed was a microwave! Sure, she didn't have her priorities in order—but hey, if it weren't for Martha, no one would've eaten! Even though my husband urged me to take it easy at times, he still marveled at my ability to pack twice as much stuff into each day. Could it be the Martha in me was a gift, provided I used it for good and not guilt?

Soon after, Martha's story came up at my Bible study. My teacher, Kris, said, "Wouldn't you love going to her house for dinner? She'd make everything lovely and delicious—the original Martha Stewart!" Kris asked how many of us identified with Martha, and three-fourths of us raised our hands. At least I'm not alone.

We made a list of Martha's personality traits. In her favor, she had the gift of hospitality. She opened her heart and her home to Jesus. She had a servant's heart and a teachable spirit. When Jesus corrected her, she received his criticism. She was a woman of action whose biggest shortcoming was her self-righteous complaining about her sister, Mary.

In Luke 10:41, Jesus counters Martha's frustration with Mary by saying, "Martha, Martha, you are worried and bothered about so many things; but only a few things are necessary, really only one, for Mary has chosen the good part" (NASB).

Jesus never told her to *be* Mary; he told her not to worry about unimportant things. Jesus didn't order Mary to help Martha, but he didn't order Martha to stop serving and sit at his feet, either. Preparing the meal was a valuable service, but Martha's grumbling detracted from her good deed.

Martha wasn't so bad—she just needed an attitude adjustment! And so did I. Being able to juggle many things at once gave me the opportunity to serve many people. Yet I had a tendency to go overboard. I'd been a hot-line counselor for a crisis pregnancy center, but before long, perhaps because of my inability to say or understand the word *no,* I became director of education at the center and soon was busy speaking on behalf of the unborn at schools and churches. That's a Martha for you!

However, I finally questioned my motives. As I left our baby daughter, Brittany, with a girlfriend for the third time that week, a wave of conviction hit me. I'd resigned from teaching high school to raise our daughter. Yet here I was, running all over town—even if it was for a good cause.

But after that convicting moment, I asked God to do some pruning. I shared my concerns with the center and decided to resign. After a year away, I've returned to the hot line at a crisis pregnancy center, but my late-evening shift doesn't conflict with my role as wife and mother.

Even so, my attitude continues to be adjusted. My

daughter and I had lunch with a good friend, "Mary," and her daughters. She asked if we would prefer white or wheat, crunchy or creamy. That was it—peanut-butter sandwiches! And even though they weren't cut in little triangles with a fruit garnish, they tasted great, and we had a lovely time.

That was another revelation for me! A peanut-butter sandwich served with loving calm tastes a lot better than any made-from-scratch, knock-yourself-out meal prepared by a stressed-out Martha. And the point of having guests over is not to win the clean-kitchen award but to enjoy their company. Forsaking fellowship for a sink full of dishes was selfish of me. Just let 'em soak!

I realize I'll always be a Martha. After wrestling with her for almost a decade, I've learned, as Popeye said, "I yam what I yam." But rather than striving to be Mary, I can strive to be the best of Martha—the transformed Martha with the servant's heart and the teachable spirit. I know now the Lord has given me certain strengths and weaknesses—and depending on how I handle it, my busyness can be both.

For a change, why not throw a "reverse birthday party" on your birthday? Bob and I contacted a church-sponsored organization that houses street people in Washington and found out what each person most wanted. We then gave them gifts in honor of his birthday and shared our faith and the importance of having Jesus Christ in your life. Many of these people have now become Christians!

ELIZABETH DOLE

TEN YEARS AGO, WHEN I WAS A NEW BRIDE AND THE "adopted mom" of thirty-eight high school youth-group kids, I used to run around crazily before the teens arrived, vacuuming our apartment and making sure all surfaces were dust- and clutter-free. I'd make homemade brownies or another delicious dessert to make sure we'd always have munchies available. After several months of watching this "busy activity" three times a week, my ever-wise husband, Jeff, said quietly, "You know, hon, they're coming to see us, not the house. And they come because there's love here."

That sweet—and much-needed—reminder helped me to realize that I didn't have to be "the perfect homemaker" to have guests over. I could relax more; and instead of spending so much time slaving in the kitchen, I could whip up a batch of popcorn to fill always-hungry teen tummies.

If you want people to feel "kindly welcome" in your home, try these suggestions—from the "grandmas" of the hospitality world.

Realize You Don't Have to Be Suzy Homemaker to Have People Over

DENISE TURNER

My grandmother was the most hospitable person I have ever known. People dropped by her house every day for a piece of her home-baked coconut cake. When people drop by my house, I'm usually not home—and I don't even know how to bake coconut cake. That used to bother me until the day I caught my grandmother sneaking a cake mix into her kitchen cupboard. "These things are every bit as moist as mine," she said with a giggle. "The only reason I didn't use them fifty years ago is because nobody had thought them up."

Why was Grandmother such a wonderful hostess? The reasons probably have little to do with the meals she prepared and everything to do with who she was. Here's some sage hospitality wisdom I've gleaned from her:

1. Grandmother was not the world's most perfect home-maker. She wasn't a trained gourmet cook either. So you might as well forget about getting elaborate recipes from her. Instead, concentrate on her favorite tips, like "Cook with the freshest fruits and vegetables you can get" or "Simple, basic foods are best."

2. Grandmother was genuinely happy to see everyone— and thus everyone seemed to congregate on her doorstep. The perennial "open house" may be out of style today. Yet we can still dedicate our homes to God and carry on Grandmother's attitude of love for people.

3. Grandmother's gift of hospitality did not depend on large amounts of money. This was evidenced by the fact that she always insisted she liked the chicken backs best. Of course, the wealthier you are, the more elegant your entertaining style can be. But how many of your friends genuinely prefer caviar to vegetables and dip?

4. Grandmother did make the best gingerbread cookies in the world. However, most people remember the gingery smell of Grandmother's house more clearly than the exact taste of the cookies. It was an atmosphere she created that people remember with fondness.

Of course, it's impossible to re-create the "good old days," and we probably wouldn't be happy living Grandmother's life, even if we could. But we can combine the best of the old with the best of the new.

Grandmother's special brand of hospitality is summed up in an old Shaker motto that says, "We make you kindly welcome." The Shakers follow these simple rules of hospitality: Keep hot food hot and cold food cold—and always give your hands to work and your heart to God.

Some ideas never go out of style.

WHEN YOU THINK OF ENTERTAINING, WHAT IMAGES COME into your mind? A table set with the best crystal-and-china fare? a beautiful flower arrangement? a buffet that could be pictured in a magazine spread?

If you want to entertain with style but you don't have much time to prepare, try these easy tips by Jane Johnson Struck for simply elegant dining.

And if you worry about those "silent moments"—the times when the table gets quiet and no one knows what to say—try Kathy Bence's tips for some great conversation starters. You and your guests will be chattering away in no time!

ENTERTAIN SIMPLY, BUT WITH STYLE
JANE JOHNSON STRUCK

- 💡 CLASSY FIESTA Bring out your best for your friends. Don't save your best crystal, china, and silver (if you have them) only for holidays or that rare "the-boss-is-coming-for-dinner" dinner. Everyday dishes can be just as festive if you use colorful placemats, a striking centerpiece, or creative napkin folding. And don't forget the candles!

- 💡 ADOPT A THEME Build your party around a specific theme. Take your cue from the season or the menu. Then decorate accordingly. At your local library, you'll find entertaining guides filled with useful and inexpensive ideas for delightful decorating schemes. "I like to add something of interest to each party I give," my friend Dede says. It may be a personalized gift at each place setting or some other unique touch to make the evening memorable.

- 💡 PLACES, PLEASE Use place cards to prevent that "sit anywhere" confusion. Designate seating arrangements with small cards—white for formal occasions, colored for casual. Or tie them in with your party theme.

MIX 'N' MATCH Stay flexible. You may not have enough bread-and-butter plates to serve eight, or twelve matching dinner plates. Mix and match with an eye to color and pattern, and you'll set a pretty and interesting table.

PUT GUESTS AT EASE
KATHY BENCE

 FOCUS ON YOUR GUESTS How you regard others can make a difference. When talking to someone, concentrate less on what she may think of you and more on getting to know her. Call each person by name so she feels accepted.

 TASK SMARTS Let shy guests help you prepare a salad or set the table to allow them time to overcome their nervousness. You may want to ask someone gifted in drawing others out to talk to the most uncomfortable guests.

 RELAX YOUR SETTING Create a comfortable setting. Build a fire in the fireplace. Put soothing music on the stereo. Use green plants to "soften" your living room. Less formal surroundings help visitors relax.

 EASY TREATS Offer easy-to-eat hors d'oeuvres so your guests have something to do while getting acquainted.

 BREAK THE ICE If you don't know your guests, plan some simple activities: a drive in the country, a walk through your neighborhood, a project everyone enjoys.

 THE KEY: TALKING AND LISTENING If conversation lags, ask: Where did you grow up? Tell me about your job. What was the highlight of this past year? What do you enjoy doing? What's the best book you've been reading lately? Most people want to be included in the conversation but may not know how to open up. Set an example by sharing freely from your own life. Then listen carefully as your quiet friends begin to follow your lead.

MAGAZINES STREWN ACROSS THE COFFEE TABLE. BATHROOM cabinets stuffed to overflowing. The hall closet you wish you hadn't opened, because now you can't get it closed. The junk mail that proliferates on your kitchen counter. Clothes in three different sizes in your closet (you just *know* someday you'll squeeze back into that smaller size!).

Clutter. All of us deal with it on a daily basis—and wish we had a better way to control it. But before you let your clutter get the best of you, try these great suggestions from a woman who fought clutter—and won!

Control Clutter

AMANDA LLOYD

"I can't find anything in this house!" My husband's admonition crushed me. But deep inside I was just as frustrated with our cluttered lifestyle as he.

Suddenly, pots, pans, dishes, and casseroles piled up on every available surface. My mission: to get our kitchen organized. As the cabinets emptied, my husband retreated to the living room for safety.

Three hours later, sweating with a jubilant glow, I had accomplished my mission. Boxes of unused kitchen and household equipment now sat in our basement. And amazingly, several empty kitchen cabinets also appeared. The following day I loaded the boxes into my car and headed for the resale shop.

If you, too, need to control the clutter in your home, here's how:

1. Be selective. Being aware of my clutter downfall is half the battle; resisting temptation is the other half. Before you bring another thing into your house, think about its usefulness and where you'll store it. Decide if you really need it or simply want it.

2. Live with less. Once you decide to be selective, you've taken the first step toward a simpler lifestyle. But if you honestly try to live with less, you'll be surprised at how your battle with clutter can become more manageable.

On a rampage through my dresser one morning, I counted eight "around the house" T-shirts. I thought about it, then packed up five. I can manage with three just fine.

3. Pretend you're moving. Go through closets, cupboards, or the basement and ask yourself, Would I really want to pack this up, load it on the truck, unpack it, then find a new place for it? The answer is frequently no.

Each time I am overcome with the desire to clear out clutter, I grab a stack of paper bags to fill with the offending items. Once a bag is full, I staple it shut so I'm not tempted to take things out. Then it's off to the "Central Clearing Zone" of my basement. When my pile reaches the ten-bag limit, it's off to the charity shop.

At times I do dream of moving to a bigger home with "loads of storage space." But then I have to get a grip on myself and remember a bigger house would only mean more clutter.

4. Don't do it alone. Talk over a clutter-control strategy with your spouse and children; get their ideas. Friends, too, can be a great source of organizational tips. If you don't have a knack for organization, ask a friend who seems to have the natural ability to drop by your house and offer her insights. Compulsive organizers thrive on this kind of opportunity.

5. Think before you act. Before you go on an organizational stampede, sit down in the middle of the room you're about to attack, and list all the areas that need organization. Then dream up ways to organize. Let your plan stew for a few weeks, make changes, and *then* begin organizing.

DO YOU EVER FEEL AS IF YOU'RE THE ONLY ONE WHO'S really working at home? Maybe your kids disappear when it's time to do the dishes or take out the garbage. Or your husband invites his boss over for dinner, then settles down for five hours of television instead of helping you with the preparations.

Before you start inwardly (or outwardly) fuming, remember this: Just because your family isn't offering to help doesn't necessarily mean they aren't willing. Try these tips.

ALLOW YOUR KIDS TO HELP
KATHY BENCE

 CHILDREN UNDER TEN CAN
- pick flowers for the table;
- choose and arrange seating;
- draw creative placecards for guests;
- set the table;
- butter the bread;
- give their opinions about the menu;
- serve appetizers (if they aren't spillable);
- crack and beat eggs;
- create centerpieces (with supervision);
- greet guests at the door;
- knead dough in a child-sized pan.

 CHILDREN OVER TEN CAN
- help elderly guests to the table;
- cook with simple recipes;
- assemble easy-to-prepare hors d'oeuvres;
- act as host/hostess or waiter/waitress;
- hang up coats;
- clear the dishes after the meal;
- do anything on the list for "Children under Ten."

By allowing your children to help, you develop their sense of self-worth and responsibility—and give them cherished memories.

GET YOUR HUSBAND TO HELP WITHOUT BEING A NAG!
ELAINE K. MCEWAN-ADKINS

💡 BECOME SHERLOCK HOLMES Try to figure out why your husband isn't doing his share. Perhaps he wasn't raised to believe housework was his responsibility. Maybe he feels inadequate, incompetent, or he's stressed out from work. Do some detective work.

💡 RELAX YOUR STANDARDS Usually, we want a job done *now*, and we want it done *our* way. So, even when our husband does manage to help, we end up criticizing his work. The answer? Keep our mouth shut!

💡 EVERYBODY LOVES A COMPLIMENT Compliment the work your husband does—and don't redo the job when he's done. Husbands often feel as helpless regarding household tasks as we feel when faced with an oil change or flat tire. Remember, doing anything new takes practice.

💡 DINNER OUT—WITH A PURPOSE Take your husband out to dinner, and discuss the issue of workload in a quiet, relaxed atmosphere. Never ambush him when you're both exhausted. Pose the problem as you see it, and brainstorm solutions. The answer may not necessarily be a fifty-fifty split of household chores.

💡 A SWAP A DAY If possible, hire someone to do the jobs neither of you likes to do. Or swap some chores. For instance, I prefer mowing the lawn to cooking meals. My husband agreed to cook several evenings per week—and we're both happier. Enlist the help of your children, too!

SUSAN, A YOUNG MOM OF TWO, IS ONE OF THE MOST
hospitable women I know. Although she and her husband, Dan,
both work in ministry and have few extra funds, they invite
college students over each Sunday for dinner. After school their
home is buzzing with kids hungry for a snack, a listening ear, or
a hug. Susan and Dan's "open-door policy" has extended the
love of Christ to many neighbors and the larger community.

If you think hospitality has to be an "organized event," think
again. And then step on over to Susan and Dan's. I'm sure
they'll have some cookies and a smile ready just for you.

Such an "open-door policy" is what the next story is all about.

Adopt an Open-Door Policy

LAURETTA PATTERSON

I recently walked into a local bookstore and found myself in
what appeared to be the fairy-tale section. A collection of
books on gracious entertaining lined the shelves. One book
cover in particular caught my eye: There stood the hostess,
elegantly dressed. Behind her sat a table laden with master-
pieces for the eye and palate. The decorations? Her own. The
fresh produce and herbs? From her garden, of course.

For many of us such a triumph is like something from the
enchanted forest. We live instead in a world of plastic tablecloths, Ground Beef Delight, and wilted-flower arrangements.
Surely there's a lot to be said for gracious living—but as
Christian women, we are called to more than the pursuit of
social niceties. Our hospitality should serve the lonely and
broken of this world as well as build up believers to work for
the kingdom.

Look at the hospitality shown by Publius, a chief official
on the island on which the apostle Paul landed, shipwrecked
and snake-bitten: "He [Publius] welcomed us to his home
and for three days entertained us hospitably. . . . They hon-

ored us in many ways and when we were ready to sail, they furnished us with the supplies we needed" (Acts 28:7-10). Publius couldn't help but notice the disheveled band of shipwrecked sailors and prisoners that showed up at his door. But the ship-wrecked ones near us may not be so obvious. Surely the children of today's culture are among the adrift. Left to fend for themselves in a disintegrating world, they long for the safety of a friendly face or a place to belong.

I answered my doorbell one day to find a very earnest, wide-eyed little boy perched on my doorstep. With a quavery voice, he said, "My name's Billy, and I don't have *any* friends!" Soon my three boys had made him a regular member of their wooden-sword-fighting gang in our backyard.

But many of the lonely ones around us will not be so forthright in stating their needs. However, if our eyes are open, we'll notice them. Is there a single parent close by who needs a touch of relief and encouragement? How about an elderly neighbor who's fearful and lonely, or a disabled and isolated person desperate for contact with a friendly face?

It may not be only the lost and unbelieving who need a safe harbor. We're to "do good to all people, especially to those who belong to the family of believers" (Gal. 6:10), and to "show hospitality to such men [fellow Christians] so that we may work together for the truth" (3 John 1:8). Christians get worn out, too, and need an oasis where they can be loved, restored, fed, and prayed for.

We can open wide the doors of our homes and declare, "Come on in! Be part of the family. Join the inner circle!"

> *My father's mother, Grandmother Hill, was a great encouragement to me. She would have a full-course meal ready for me, even if I arrived at her home at midnight! When I'm older, I hope I'm as close to my children and grandchildren in heart and locale.*
>
> SUSAN ASHTON

There is something profoundly intimate about being "let in" to another person's home. If you would ring my doorbell today and pop in for a cup of coffee, you would definitely know me in a different way than if you had met me in public. You would see the scattered photos of babies, relatives, and children and know I value a strong family life; all manner of Legos and castles under construction would speak of the "creative disorder" rampant in our home; a hint of doggy odor in the entryway would alert you to the presence of our beloved (but ill-mannered) Frances the Mutt. You'd know the books we're currently reading because you'd find them in the bathroom. Very quickly you'd discover that we postpone fixing things, that I love garage-sale finds, and that a picture of a laughing Christ hangs prominently over the whole enterprise. "Welcome to my place" are words that invite intimacy, and I speak them now far more easily after experiencing loving hospitality myself.

What about entertaining? What do we do with folks once we've welcomed them in? Sometimes we think of entertaining as creating a sparkling agenda for our guests; we feel compelled to spotlight our own strengths. But at the core of hospitable entertaining lies a willingness to share both the joys and the heartaches of life. Who has time to sterilize life into some sort of antiseptic condition in order to entertain? Make your guests part of the family, and they will truly feel at home.

But let's be honest. The biggest hitch in showing hospitality is lack of time. Each day has too few hours to get basic life maintenance done, much less reach out to someone else. It's reassuring to remember that we are not the Messiah— Jesus is! That perspective comes from regular times spent with the Lord as well as upholding the Sabbath commanded by God but ignored by most of Christendom. Take the time to be restored in body, mind, and spirit, and reaching out will be much more joyful.

Remember, too, that hospitality giving has its seasons. A friend once attended a talk by a woman known for her welcoming heart and open home. After listening to the speaker urge involvement in caring for those in pain, my friend asked, "How do I begin to open my home? I have three small children, and I'm overwhelmed most of the time."

"Oh, my dear," said the speaker. "Your home is open exactly the way it needs to be right now—to a husband and three tiny children who need your full attention. There will come another season in your life, and then you'll be able to reach out differently!"

Focus on your guests, not your home. You don't need to cook elaborate food or have a living room that could appear in Better Homes and Gardens *to be hospitable.*

RAMONA CRAMER TUCKER

The body of Christ is meant to function as a healthy unit, taking into account the seasons, gifts, and limitations of each member. Pooling our resources with other members of the body means we can be hospitable far beyond our own abilities. A church filled with hospitality givers can be a potent force for Christ and a guard against individual burnout. What an opportunity we have to affect the world through the corporate hospitality we give as a church!

Today's world presents a dizzying array of options for women; we may be stretched in ways our mothers could only guess at. But the ministry of welcoming others into our home and life remains a call we must not ignore. No matter the season of life or the limitations of schedule, we can ask the Lord for a heart that's open and the eyes to see those who crave a resting place.

WHEN YOU HEAR SOMEONE TALK ABOUT HOSPITALITY, DO you inwardly groan? Do you think of all the commitments you have and wonder when you'd ever find time to entertain? In such times it's good to remember the difference between entertaining and hospitality. *Entertaining* focuses on material things—the right food, the proper table—while *hospitality* focuses on people. Hospitality is, simply, loving people, being available and ready to listen to them.

No matter whether you're single, a career woman, a stay-at-home mom, a working mom, a widow, all of us are called by Christ to be hospitable. And it's not as hard as you think. Here's why:

Practice Hospitality on the Run

RACHAEL CRABB WITH JANE JOHNSON STRUCK

"Today we're more concerned about locking our doors than bringing people into our homes," says Rachael Crabb, wife of Christian psychologist Larry Crabb and author of *The Personal Touch* (NavPress), a practical book on biblical hospitality. "Yet even in the end times, when the 'love of most will grow cold,' we still need to be hospitable to believers and non-Christians alike."

Rachael has had a wealth of experience in practicing the ministry of hospitality. "When I grew up, we always had missionaries staying with us," explains Rachael. "And Larry and I have had a very open home. When our children were young, we'd have weekly neighborhood potlucks where we'd alternate homes. And our boys enjoyed being around all the different people. What a mind stretcher it is to sit around your table and hear others share how God is working in their lives!"

Rachael readily admits that despite her love of hospitality, she does hate housework. "People who read my book send me easy recipes because they know how I hate to cook," she says with a laugh. "Fortunately, there aren't any rules that apply. Hospitality isn't about linen tablecloths; it's about giving—giving of yourself to others. I like to say, 'People are more important—so let's have a good time!'"

Rachael is quick to emphasize that "other-centeredness"—not organizational skills or a *House Beautiful* home—is the necessary ingredient for effective outreach.

"It's easy to be overwhelmed at the prospect of offering hospitality," Rachael says. "We all feel overscheduled at times. But even the most harried woman can give of herself in small but effective ways. The key is to care—to let others see a bit of Christ shining through."

Some nonthreatening methods of practicing hospitality don't even need to take place in the home, suggests Rachael. "You're never too busy to drop a postcard to someone who needs encouraging," she says. And to help ease entertaining jitters, Rachael recommends teaming up with someone more experienced to host that first get-together.

"Christian women just don't have a choice about whether or not they'll be hospitable," says Rachael. "It's a biblical command. Scripture tells us that in the last days, people will be lovers of themselves. We, as Christians, are called to be givers instead. And that's what hospitality is all about."

THINK IT OVER

Does your home need organization? less clutter? Do you need more of your family's help? Do you need to focus less on your home and food and more on your guests? How long has it been since you were hospitable to someone in need?

Pray, asking God to reveal to you the areas that need to change in your home and hospitality style. Choose one area to concentrate on. Brainstorm some solutions; then implement one or two over the next month.

Marriage

Marriage is a series of phases,
where we can fall in and out of love.
During the times we're not feeling in love,
we must hold fast to our wedding vows and
trust God to preserve the relationship.

SUSAN ASHTON

HOW'S YOUR MARRIAGE WORKING?

WHEN my husband, Jeff, and I first met, we were as different as anyone could imagine. Our premarital personality tests told us point-blank that we two shouldn't even be friends, much less marriage partners.

I was a "schedule maniac"; he was a free spirit who didn't mind if his youth group kids called at 2 A.M. I liked to dress up in velvet and lace and didn't even own jeans; Jeff's classiest attire was a white T-shirt, black jeans, and cowboy boots. I loved to cook and sew; he preferred action movies and racing his Monte Carlo.

After eleven years of marriage, we're still poles apart in personality, but we've discovered how good those differences can be. I make sure the bills get paid on time and houseguests get fed; Jeff makes sure everything mechanical runs perfectly and lights up any atmosphere with the right touch of humor. In fact, our uniqueness makes our house a place where people of varying backgrounds can feel right "at home."

Who says that differences in marriage can't be reconciled—and that we can't have fun along the way? That's what this chapter is about.

WHAT KEEPS A MARRIAGE HAPPY THROUGHOUT THE YEARS?
How do couples survive the tough times—and manage to keep
their marriages alive and growing? When we asked Carole
Mayhall, who with husband, Jack, speaks, counsels, and
teaches other couples about marriage nationwide, what she
sees as the secrets to a healthy marriage, here's what she said:

Keep Your Marriage Happy

CAROLE MAYHALL

What's the secret to being happily married? Here are eight
key ingredients to keeping your marriage healthy.

1. Use the right "super glue." Happy couples share a
commitment to God. When a wife can share the deepest
things of her heart with her husband, there is true contentment and lasting joy. "God is the glue that holds two
people together," our minister once said. When other factors in a marriage are weak, this one—a mutual love for
God and desire to serve him—can keep two people determined to work toward a relationship that reflects God's
love and power.

2. Be friends as well as lovers. Most women rate "love
and affection" number one when they list what they desire
most from marriage. Most men rate "companionship" at
the top—even above sex. Doing things together—reading
quietly, driving in friendly silence, sharing a joke, or playing tennis together—is vital. Happy couples *play* together,
enjoy what the other enjoys, and find things to laugh about
together.

One man told us that his marriage took on a new dimen-
sion when he bought a motorcycle! His wife—a short
woman who couldn't reach the ground when she sat on the
back of it—loved to seek out unusual restaurants. So she

researched places to go, gave him directions, and away they went!

Happy couples also build each other up. First Peter 3:7 tells husbands to "be considerate as you live with your wives, and treat them with respect." A wife is commanded to respect her husband (Eph. 5:33). The Greek word for *respect* also implies adoring, enjoying, appreciating, and preferring him (*Amplified Bible*). In other words, happy couples are best friends who march at the head of the other's parade, who are the president of the other's fan club, and who are cheerleaders for their spouse. They know the truth of 1 Corinthians 13:7 (TLB): "If you love someone, you will be loyal to him no matter what the cost. You will always believe in him, always expect the best of him, and always stand your ground in defending him."

> *I wouldn't trade a moment of my wife Mary's unconditional love for anything in this world. And I can't wait to see what lies around the bend for Mary and me on this wild and wonderful ride called marriage.*
>
> CLIFF SCHIMMELS

3. Tune in to pillow talk. A speaker once said, "The goal of communication isn't mouth to ear (surface talk) or mind to mind (facts and ideas). It isn't even heart to heart (feelings). The *real* goal is soul to soul—the ability to openly share joys, successes, hurts, dreams, and fears without rejection."

Happy couples make the time and effort to explore each other's souls. But for that kind of communication to exist, each partner must understand and accept each other's differences.

I saw that in my parents' marriage. Occasionally Dad would say, "I don't need a radio in the car when Mother is along," or "I talk in my sleep because that's the only time I can get a word in edgewise." But then he'd grin at my mom with love and tenderness. His teasing never had an edge to it. We *knew* he not only understood her but accepted and *respected* her.

Marriage is designed to teach us true intimacy. For this to happen, thoughts and feelings must flow freely. Happy couples keep striving for a deeper level of communication throughout their marriage.

4. Refuse to win. One gauge of marital happiness is how effectively couples deal with anger, conflict, and frustration. When one spouse sets out to "win" alone, both spouses lose. Instead, happy couples solve their conflicts so they *both* win—with a mutually satisfying resolution. They're also essentially good forgivers—they don't hold grudges. Happy couples work through the majors, shrug off the minors, and are mature enough to know the difference.

5. Stay true blue. Happy couples are faithful. Fidelity was a "given" for the 100 couples Dr. Catherine Johnson, author of *Lucky in Love,* interviewed about the secret to their happiness. "For them, being faithful to each other was not what made a marriage happy—it was what made a marriage possible in the first place."

6. Make room for change. God wants everyone to change, grow, develop—and marriage is one of his best instruments for that! Happy couples realize that in marriage "change is the name of the game." They see the truth in Proverbs 27:17: "As iron sharpens iron, so one man sharpens another." They realize that when two lives rub together daily, sparks can fly. But as changes occur, each person becomes more Christlike.

One difference Jack and I encountered in our marriage was in the way we expressed affection. I came from a demonstrative family, and when Jack didn't hug or kiss me as often as I expected, I thought he didn't love me and became silent and depressed. As Jack began to realize how important affection was to me, he worked hard at becoming more demonstrative. On the other hand, I began to realize he expressed his love through his caregiving, tenderness, and acceptance—and I began appreciating his ways more and demanding my way less.

All I know is that God gave me this man—and this man only—to honor, to cherish, to enjoy. And instead of fretting about what he is not, I can celebrate what he is.

ELIZABETH CODY NEWENHUYSE

7. Keep the flame burning. Happy couples know the value of romance. Sex is part of romance, but touching, holding hands, meeting eyes across a room, winking, or smiling over a "family joke" also are part of it. Happy couples realize the importance of making time together—apart from the children, if they have them—a priority.

We heard one prominent marriage counselor tell an engaged couple two things that would ensure the success of their marriage: budgeting the time and money for a marriage retreat every year and dating. Our goal is a date once a week, but if that is impossible, once every other week is a minimum. Couples with good marriages make time to enhance the romance in their relationship.

8. Act as a team. Happy couples realize that marriage is a team sport, not a competition. Each carries the other when he or she is down and supports the other spouse when he or she is weak. Happy couples don't lead separate lives under one roof but refer to "our money," "our children," "our home," and "our plans." They have the "one flesh" relationship the Bible describes and have grasped the significance of 1 Peter 3:8: "Finally, all of you, live in harmony with one another; be sympathetic, love as brothers, be compassionate and humble."

HAVE YOU EVER ASKED YOUR HUSBAND A QUESTION ONLY
to receive the male "grunt"? Sometimes that monosyllable means
"Leave me alone. I need a brain-rinse of television"; other times it
may mean "I'm not really listening, but I know you need to talk, so
go ahead"; other times it may mean "Whatever you want is fine
with me." But how do we go beyond those one-word answers to
real communication without feeling like we're dragging conversation out of him? Here's how to *really* talk to your man.

Talk to Your Husband

EILEEN SILVA KINDIG

Do you long for deep, meaningful communication within
marriage? If so, try these ideas:

Verbalize for him. Although most women consider themselves more empathetic than their mates, exhaustive studies at the University of Arizona have shown that men
equal women in understanding and compassion—it's just
that men aren't as comfortable showing it. Women with
successful marriages understand this and gently lead their
men down the path of open dialogue.

One of the most intimate conversations my husband and I
ever shared was about redecorating our house. We had just
moved into our home, and my husband spent every spare
moment replacing floor coverings, wallpaper, and coun-
tertops. For two months we argued until I finally realized that
behind all the activity loomed my husband's loud message:
"I feel overwhelmed here and can't rest until this is finished!"

Once I realized this and put it into words for him, he was
able to tell me his dreams for the place. This led to sharing
about our childhood homes and how our house reflected who
we are individually and as a couple.

Talk, look, and listen. Listening for unspoken messages isn't the only way to lovingly help husbands open up. There's also something called *reflection:* repeating what a person said, without interrupting, criticizing, or analyzing. Unconsciously, I used this tool when my husband and I sorted through our feelings about the house.

"I've got to get this old flooring off. . . . Look at this mess!" he moaned.

"Honey, it sounds like you feel pressured," I responded.

He stopped ripping lineoleum and looked up, surprised. "That's what I've been trying to tell you!"

Normally I would have cut him off. But by listening and reflecting, I finally stopped to hear him out, understand his feelings, and share my own more rationally. I also learned that, despite the words I'd been spewing for the past eight weeks, my real message was just as hidden as his. Behind my anger and frustration lay the fear that the house was robbing us of time together.

Speak the language of love. Because we women are usually more verbal than our husbands, we also run the risk of "flooding" them with self-disclosure. Men don't really want to hear every little nuance or have conversations repeated verbatim. They want the *gist* of the thing. We cannot reasonably expect to communicate deeply all the time; we just need to know that we *can*.

My husband and I look forward to our nightly three-mile walk. We laugh, argue, analyze, even cry, but always connect in some elemental way. When, for some reason, we don't take this time, we begin to feel distanced. Why? Because intimacy takes time and dedication. It's a constant process, and sometimes we're less than graceful at it. But if we remember that meaningful dialogue requires four ingredients—trust, acceptance, respect, and caring—and use them as our guidelines, the answer to "Can we talk?" will be a resounding "Yes!"

WITH ALL THE BARRIERS TO FRIENDSHIP—TIME, CHILDREN, and personalities, to mention a few—it's no wonder many married couples have a difficult time cultivating friendships. Finding friends may not be easy, but the benefits to your marriage are well worth the search. Based on a variety of women's experiences, here are some tips for building and maintaining marriage-enhancing friendships:

ACTIVELY SEEK FRIENDSHIPS
JANIS LONG HARRIS

💡 BE ACTIVE Don't wait for friendships to "happen." Follow the example of Leslie and Peter, who realized that after several moves they didn't have any close friends anymore. "We picked ten couples and invited them over, one by one, over a period of six months. It was a trial-and-error process—a lot of the couples didn't pan out as friends, but some did."

💡 SHARE AND SHARE ALIKE Seek out friendships with people who share your values and interests. Shared beliefs, whether they relate to religion, child rearing, or social concerns, can draw people together in friendships as well as marriage. But just attending church services, for example, may not be enough to spark warm friendships. Volunteering on a committee or joining a small group can provide a niche within which deep friendships can develop.

💡 WATER YOUR FRIENDSHIP Good friendships require care and feeding, so don't take your existing friendships for granted. If your friends (particularly singles, who may feel "left out of the loop" if you've recently married) haven't contacted you in a while, take the initiative and suggest plans for getting together. Send them a note telling them what their friendship means to you.

BE SENSITIVE Be sensitive to your mate's friendship needs. Like virtually every other issue in marriage, developing satisfying friendships requires compromise. Paul and I don't always agree about which couples we'd like to get together with or, in some cases, whether we'd like to spend time with friends at all. But we're both happier when we mutually demonstrate that we care how the other feels.

 ALLOW FOR INDIVIDUALITY Don't expect all your friendships to be mutual. Natalie and Rick have been married for fifteen years. They met and dated in college and have a number of mutual friends. Natalie's closest friend, however, was a woman she had known since childhood. After they stopped trying to force a four-way friendship beyond an occasional get-together, Natalie and Emily were freed to enjoy their own continued friendship. "Emily and I remained best friends despite the fact that our husbands are just socially polite," explains Natalie.

 REALIZE LIFE GOES ON Mourn your lost friendships and move on. Paul and I value our friendships enough that when we lose one through a move or change, we tend to sit around and talk about how much fun we'd be having if only we could be with Jim and Susie. There's nothing wrong with mourning a friendship, unless it prevents you from making new ones.

 EXPECT THE UNPREDICTABLE Remain open to unexpected friendships. Although chances are you and your spouse are more likely to become friends with people with whom you share a neighborhood, age bracket, church, or work situation, friendships aren't necessarily predictable. One young couple I know of became best friends with a couple almost twenty years their senior—despite few outward common circumstances. Their advice to other couples: Be open to serendipity. If you stick too rigidly to your categories, you can miss some great new friendships.

I'LL NEVER FORGET THE FIRST DAY MY HUSBAND, JEFF, MADE me feel cherished. We'd been married three weeks when we took a group of high schoolers to a roller-skating rink for some evening fun. While I was skating, a local teen whizzed around me twice, knocking me down. But before I could struggle to my feet, my "knight on roller skates" swooped in and carried me to safety. At that moment I knew I not only was loved but *cherished*.

What things make you feel cherished? What things make your spouse feel cherished? Here's how to find out:

Cherish Your Spouse

CAROLE MAYHALL

Somehow over the years, while we still love our spouse, we often forget the importance of *cherishing* each other.

The truth is, men and women define *cherish* differently. To me, being cherished means feeling cared for and protected and treasured. I know my husband, Jack, loves me. But I feel cherished when he says, "I don't want you driving in this fog—I'll take you," or "Let me carry that—it's too heavy for you."

But Jack would probably give grudging assent to "being cared for," raise an eyebrow at "protection," and look bewildered at "treasured." What really makes him feel special may be a little less predictable. As the Amplified version of Ephesians 5:33 says, "Let the wife see that she respects and reverences her husband—that she notices him, regards him, honors him, prefers him, venerates and esteems him; and that she defers to him, praises him, and loves and admires him exceedingly."

Sounds good, doesn't it? But how in the world do we *do* it? Try these action steps.

1. Pray for wisdom. The God who promises us wisdom (James 1:5) will give us understanding. Take two or three weeks to concentrate on praying for special insight and wisdom for your particular situation. Look up verses on wisdom and pray about them.

2. Ask. Because God made each man unique, I doubt anyone can tell how men in general feel cherished, honored, or appreciated. Each of us needs to determine *how* our own husband feels about those things by asking him, talking to others, and repeating others' thinking to get his feedback.

3. Build an atmosphere of caring. One way to create a climate of acceptance and appreciation is through praise and admiration. Write down the qualities you respect and love in your husband, and make a point to share one each week in detail. Avoid put-downs and discouraging remarks, both in public and in private.

4. Study. Most husbands have a difficult time verbalizing the information you seek, so study your husband's response to things you do. For Jack, "I love you" spelled out with M&M's on his desk and a red cutout heart among his shirts are causes for a quiet grin, but he feels more cherished when I make an apple pie or cancel a social engagement when he is peopled out.

5. Think deeds. Words are important, but for the significant men in my life, cherishing is heard more loudly through actions. Most of us make the mistake of projecting our own preferences on others. We reason that if something makes us feel treasured, it makes everyone feel that way, and we act accordingly. Many times women want *presence,* and men want *deeds*.

While the word *love* makes up the marriage painting, the ways we cherish each other add the beautiful strokes of color to the canvas. A marriage can probably get by without it—but how much more vivid and dynamic our marriages will be with it!

WHEN'S THE LAST TIME YOU

- rubbed your husband's feet, just because you know he likes it?
- treated him to an adventurous date?
- made his favorite dessert?
- showed up to surprise him with lunch at work?

If you can't recall the last time you've done anything like this for your spouse, try the following ideas—and then come up with your own ways to show your man he's special to you!

TREAT YOUR MAN AS SPECIAL

RAMONA CRAMER TUCKER

💡 LOVE NOTE Tuck a love note in his lunch bag or briefcase every day to remind him that no matter how his day goes, you can't wait to be at home again—together!

💡 BOYS NIGHT OUT Allow him to have a "Boys Night Out" or a "Boys Weekend." Encourage him to get together with guy friends and do something fun—a computer weekend, a dinner out at a restaurant where they can throw peanut shells on the floor and whoop it up.

💡 LIP-SNACKIN' GOOD Surprise him by making his favorite dessert or snack at the end of a long week. Or kidnap him and take him to a local ice-cream store.

💡 IT'S YOUR CHOICE Give him a movie coupon for a movie of *his* choice. (If it's my husband, I know to expect Stallone or Schwarzenegger and not a romantic movie!)

💡 WHAT A GUY! Write him an appreciation letter for something he's done around the house, accomplished at work, or just for being that all-around great guy!

SOMEWHERE OVER THE RAINBOW Make sure he gets some time to "follow his dreams"—whether it's race-car driving, skydiving, gardening, or golfing. Many men use alone time not only for relaxation but also for processing present problems and looking forward to the future.

 DREAM TOGETHER Put aside a night to cuddle up in front of your fireplace or sip some cocoa around your dinner table and dream about your future: what you'd like to do, where you'd like to go, who you want to be five years from now.

SURPRISE! When life's feeling "too predictable" or your man is stressed, try a little surprise. Rent a motel room, if you can afford it, or arrange for the kids to stay with a friend. Spending a weekend—or even a night away—with just your husband helps him to know how important he is to you.

 THE WAY TO A MAN'S HEART Ever heard this saying: "The way to a man's heart is through his stomach?" Well, it's true. And to that, I add, "and through his back." Every wife I've ever talked to says that her man loves to eat—and loves back rubs. Try one, and you'll have a very appreciative husband!

DATE NIGHTS Set aside regular date nights, and write them in ink on your calendar. Don't let anything stop you.

 CELEBRATE THE LITTLE THINGS Has your husband had a job promotion? finished cleaning out the garage? Take time to celebrate the "little things" in life. You may want to make a special cake, take him out for dinner, or hang a big Thank You or Congratulations, Hon! sign across the front door. Use your imagination—and have fun!

 XOXO Make sure your husband gets a lot of affection. Give him a morning hug; blow him a kiss out the window as he drives off for work; kiss him when he comes home from work. Smooch him when he helps you with the dishes, laundry, or mows the yard. And don't forget to kiss and hug him just for being him!

ASK ANY MARRIAGE EXPERT WHAT THE TOP PROBLEM areas in marriage are, and no doubt "in-laws" will be mentioned. Why are these relationships often fraught with tension? Combining two families can be difficult because of all the traditions, personalities, and communication styles. But as Dr. Diane Mandt Langberg says, "Communication involves two parts: first, saying what you want to get across; second, saying it in a way the other person can receive it." Through careful planning, wisdom, and a sense of humor, we *can* build a good relationship with our in-laws. Here's how:

Build a Relationship with Your In-Laws

SANDRA P. ALDRICH

At some point most married couples experience some conflict with their in-laws. Many don't realize they're marrying their spouse's entire family when they take their vows. That was a tough lesson for me to learn. My proper—and affluent—northern U.S. in-laws were horrified that their son married someone from the hills of Kentucky, and they were quick to remind me of my background.

Although my husband's parents said some rude things, I have to confess my own parents weren't thrilled about welcoming the grinning northerner who showed up to "steal" their daughter.

Although Don and I were married only sixteen years before his death, I managed to learn several lessons in the process of pursuing a better relationship with his parents. If you want to build a solid relationship with your in-laws, here are some good reminders:

Get a proper perspective. Our attitude toward any situation colors the way we see it. What if we looked at the situation from the in-law's perspective? My friend Pamela said the day her little boy developed a crush on his first-grade teacher, she understood how her mother-in-law must have felt when another woman replaced her in her son's heart. That new insight strengthened the relationship between the two women.

A good way to develop a more godly attitude toward your in-laws is to ask the Lord to help you see your in-laws through his eyes. I've discovered that the more I pray for God's perspective, the more my way of looking at things shifts for the better.

Unconditional love is much more than a tingly, romantic feeling. Tingles come and go, but real love manifests itself in the trenches of life.

DAVE AND CLAUDIA ARP

Refuse to argue. Don provided a godly example for me by refusing to get upset when one of my relatives told him how he *ought* to do something. Don wouldn't argue; he'd just smile and say something such as "Hey, thanks! I appreciate your interest." Of course, I teased him that he went ahead and did what he wanted anyway, but he reminded me it takes *two* to argue.

Schedule time with your in-laws. Don and I lived halfway between both sets of parents, so it was rare that any of them showed up unexpectedly. But we'd already decided we needed to keep in touch regularly so that they'd know they had a scheduled place in our lives and wouldn't always be wondering when they'd see us next. And it worked! Since they knew we'd either be at their house every other Sunday or have them to ours, they didn't pressure us. If your in-laws live in the same city, you may have to set some loving boundaries early, such as asking them to call before dropping in for a visit.

Guard your mouth. Remember, you never have to ask forgiveness for those sharp things you *don't* say. Instead of lashing out and putting your husband in the untenable position of having to choose between his mother and you, concentrate on showing respect. Exodus 20:12 says, "Honor your father and your mother, so that you may live long in the land the Lord your God is giving you."

Honoring your in-laws doesn't mean letting them order you around, pry into your personal finances, tell your kids to get haircuts, or rearrange your cabinets each time they visit. It means honoring their position. It also means building a relationship with your in-laws that's more friend to friend than parent to child. Your goal? Mutual respect and friendship.

Find qualities you can praise. Another friend, Phyllis, decided to handle her critical mother-in-law's visits with grace, so each time she set out to find at least two things she could sincerely compliment. One morning she gave the older woman an impromptu hug and said, "You've raised an incredible son. Thanks!" To her amazement, her mother-in-law's verbal sniping slowed down after that.

Remember, criticism destroys while encouragement builds.

Be honest with yourself. If you're always complaining about some relatively unimportant but irritating habit of your in-laws (such as leaving dishcloths in a wet clump in the sink), ask yourself what the real problem is. Is it jealousy? resentment? insecurity? a lack of forgiveness? Deal with the real problem and your relationship will likely improve.

Offer an unexpected gift. Take this advice and run with it! On Don's thirtieth birthday, I sent his mother thirty sweetheart roses with a little note that said, "I'm so glad you had a baby boy thirty years ago today."

After that, she always introduced me as "my daughter-in-law, the one who sent me the roses."

For a good gift idea, think about what your in-laws like. Perhaps they collect miniature ceramic animals, sun catchers, or strawberry-scented soaps. Or give the unexpected gift of simply inviting your in-laws out to lunch. By doing so, you show you not only care about them as in-laws but also consider them interesting people—and friends.

Good communication is the key to what we basically want as human beings—to love and be loved. We want to share our life with someone who loves us unconditionally; to grow old with a mate who values us, understands us, and makes us feel safe in sharing our deepest feelings and needs.

GARY SMALLEY

The best example. The Old Testament book of Ruth portrays the most incredible in-law relationship between two widowed women. The mother-in-law, Naomi, and her two widowed daughters-in-law, Orpah and Ruth, set out for her hometown of Bethlehem. But when they got to the border, Naomi tried to send them back, saying she had nothing to offer them. Although Orpah turned back, Ruth stayed, saying the words that became popular in wedding ceremonies during the seventies: "Where you go I will go, and where you stay I will stay. Your people will be my people and your God my God" (Ruth 1:16-17).

Think about that! Those loving words were spoken from a daughter-in-law to her mother-in-law! Naomi not only taught Ruth the customs of her new culture but also encouraged her courtship with one of Naomi's distant relatives, Boaz. Because of their warm relationship, both women benefitted—Naomi regained her family land and enjoyed security and the love of a precious grandson born to the new marriage, and Ruth gained a place in our Lord's lineage.

Most of us can learn from that account, especially when we're tempted to give in to the frustratation of working on a relationship with difficult folks. Remember the old saying to guard our tongues: "You catch more flies with honey than you do with vinegar."

WHEN MY FRIEND TISHA BECAME A CHRISTIAN SEVEN
years ago, her husband, Raul, thought she'd "gone off the deep
end." But as he settled in to wait for her Christianity to rub off, she
quietly began a prayer campaign for his soul. Day after day, Tish
would get on her knees after Raul left for work and ask God to
open Raul's heart to the gospel. She attended a weekly Bible study
during the day since Raul didn't like her attending evening or
Sunday church services. She showed her love consistently, day in
and day out, until finally he said, "You're really different. What's
all this Christianity stuff about anyway?" That Sunday night, two
years ago, Raul became a Christian. And today he's one of the
most "on fire" Christians I know—and he's gifted at friendship
evangelism.

Whether your husband is a Christian or not, we all need to
pray daily for our marriage, and for our attitude toward our
spouse. For it's when we pray that things can change—for the
good! Here's how to begin:

Pray for Your Marriage
BONNIE BUDZOWSKI

Soon after I married I realized I needed to pray daily for my
marriage. But it was easy to catch myself muttering such
things as, "Lord, help Rick throw his socks in the hamper."

I needed simple prayers based on biblical principles I
could remember and use on the busiest of days. So I started
praying, "Lord, help us to learn to cherish each other," every
day. When I started using short sentence prayers, I noticed a
real difference in my marriage. Whether my prayers grow
out of what Scripture teaches about marriage, such as "Lord,
help us to serve each other and you," or they spring from
issues and problems I'm confronting, they deepen my marriage and make it more spiritually fulfilling. Here are some

principles to help you formulate your own individual prayers:

1. Draw your prayers from Scripture. "Lord, help us to forgive each other freely" is important because we all fall short in marriage. Praying biblically gives you confidence that God will honor your prayers and shape your expectations for marriage in alignment with his Word.

2. Develop prayers that ask God to transform you and your husband into the image of Christ. I prayed, "Lord, let us treasure the things you treasure." Since prayers like this are not about things you want or consume, they will have lasting value.

3. Make sure your prayers are not complaints. Pray, "Lord, help us build up rather than tear down with our words," rather than, "Make my husband as good as I am at encouraging."

4. Make sure your prayers are practical. If they are simple rather than cumbersome or unfocused, you can find time and energy to use them daily. If they are from the heart, you will be motivated to use them. If you try a prayer and find that for some reason you are not comfortable with it, change the prayer.

These short, simple prayers have eased the tension between my goal of praying consistently for my marriage and the rush of daily duties. Sentence prayers cannot take away the need for prayer for and with our husbands. But single sentences, uttered faithfully and sincerely toward God, can have a genuine impact on your marriage.

What will your next sentence prayer be?

THINK IT OVER
In 1 Peter 4:8, God gives us this command: "Most important of all, continue to show deep love for each other, for love makes up for many of your faults" (TLB). How would you rate your attitude toward your spouse on a scale of 1 to 10 (with 1 being "not very loving," and 10 being "loving like Christ loves")? Why? Prayerfully consider your rating, then brainstorm ideas for better communication, an improved attitude, or for making your man feel treasured. As you try your strategies, be patient. Change may come slowly, but it'll be worth the effort!

Self

There is a myriad of options available about
what we can do with our life and the gifts God has
given us, but not many role models who can show us
how to juggle all these opportunities. Finding a
healthy balance between all these possibilities
is our biggest challenge.

ELISA MORGAN

How's Your "Self" Life?

WHAT ingredients would it take to make a perfect day for you? Maybe it would be staying in bed in your pajamas to read a book; working on a project you love; enjoying a day out with friends; even potty training your daughter!

As women who have numerous roles to play, sometimes we have little time to even dream about a "self" life. We're too busily involved in everyone else's life to have one of our own. But as author Ruth Senter says, "Taking time out to be alone" and to evaluate where we are and where we'd like to be is critical to our feelings about ourselves, others, and God.

When's the last time you had time alone to think, pray, enjoy, reflect, or analyze who you are and what you're becoming? This chapter will assist your thinking on subjects like contentment, turning negative thoughts into positive ones, peer pressure, scheduling—and even the importance of a laugh a day!

MY FRIEND JANA TOLD ME RECENTLY, "I DECIDED I HAVE TO stay out of the malls. Every time I go near one, I spend a couple hundred dollars on things I don't even need—and I *still* don't feel content." For Jana, that decision was the culmination of an eight-year struggle with "never enough."

And Jana isn't alone. All of us struggle, at some time in our life, with feeling content over what we have—or don't have. But in the battle for contentment, we *can* win over "never enough" and be satisfied with "what is." Here's how.

Cultivate Contentment

ELIZABETH CODY NEWENHUYSE

I know there's a lot in my life I wish I could change. I'm not miserable—but I struggle with being satisfied.

One Scripture that makes me squirm is the apostle Paul's reminder to Timothy: "But if we have food and clothing, we will be content with that" (1 Tim. 6:8). I have food, but too often it's macaroni and cheese. I have clothing, but looking through the L. L. Bean catalog brings out my most materialistic urges. I have furniture, but it resembles estate-sale treasures more than Crate and Barrel chic. Often I'd like more—and better. And that's just the beginning of my discontent.

The problem is, many of us define contentment as that ideal state of constant happiness where every problem is solved and every goal is met. But what happens when you achieve a goal? It's like yanking dandelions—you pull one, and another pops up in its place.

Ultimately, there's no true contentment apart from knowing, loving, and desiring to follow Christ. The apostle Paul always spoke of contentment in that context: "I have learned the secret of being content in any and every situation, whether well fed or hungry, whether living in plenty or in want. I can do everything through him who gives me strength" (Phil. 4:12-13).

If we're honest, most of us can't say we're content in "any and every situation." But it *is* a model to aspire to, becoming more like Paul . . . more like Christ. Here are some suggestions that may help you move closer to contentment.

> *To experience happiness we must live in this moment, savor it for what it is, not running ahead in anticipation of some future date nor lagging behind in the paralysis of the past.*
>
> LUCI SWINDOLL

USE A SPIRITUAL "MEASURING STICK"

Martha, who grew up as a preacher's kid, told me that her mother always interpreted Colossians 3:15 this way: "Let the peace of Christ be your measuring stick." If you feel uneasy about something, that may be a sign you're discontent with that situation.

About a year ago I felt very dissatisfied with my work. Every time I talked to one of my friends about my career, I was complaining. After months of prayer and soul-searching, I realized I needed to take my focus off myself and encourage others. So I took a part-time teaching position in which I could help others improve their writing. It feels right—and perhaps because I'm edging closer to what God has in mind for me.

HANG IN THERE

Is it ever possible to be discontent and still be where God wants you? Perhaps. There are times when we won't feel peaceful, when God seems indifferent. After college I went through a wandering-in-the-wilderness period. I couldn't find work; I had no friends. I came very close to taking a job out of state, but something told me, *Stay.* Not long after that, I met the man who would become my husband. God was accomplishing his purposes, even though at the time they were hidden from me.

This is where trust comes in—trust that the sovereign God is, indeed, working in your life. Have patience. And, even while you're waiting, you can . . .

GIVE THANKS

"Contentment is closely related to gratitude, a sense of feeling OK about what we have," my friend Ellen says. When we realize how much God has given us—whether we deserve it or not—we begin to move much closer to contentment. Every now and then little bursts of thankfulness sneak up on me: *What a sweet husband I've been blessed with! Thank the Lord I'm able to sleep well when I know people who suffer from insomnia.*

Look around you. What are you thankful for—a car that continues to run? a church home? good health? the gift of laughter? The possibilities are endless. When you pray, try this: Every day think of five new things to thank God for. You will never run out of ideas because God will keep supplying new ones!

ARM YOURSELF AGAINST THE SEDUCTIONS OF THE WORLD

I can think my kitchen is attractive enough—until I see a friend's newly remodeled kitchen, complete with skylights and work island. The culture makes us feel as if we *should* long for a new kitchen, a faster computer, a new job—anything other than what we have.

How do we counter such pressures? Prayer is the best armor God has given us. For example, if you know you're going to be in a situation that may stir up discontent, such as shopping or visiting a more affluent friend, pray before you go for protection from such temptations. Reread Proverbs, which has many pithy observations about character and what's important in life. Share your struggles with a friend— she'll probably love to share hers with you.

MOVE BEYOND YOURSELF

I find I'm the most discontent when I'm forever wallowing in my own needs and problems. Judy agrees, saying, "It's when I get out of myself—almost forget myself—that I'm most content. It helps to give to someone else with no expectation of reward. Doing these things gives me a feeling of balance."

A day is not ordinary or extra-ordinary in itself. It is ordinary or extra-ordinary depending on how I view it and what I choose to do with it.

RUTH SENTER

Too often our life doesn't have that balance; we're concentrating on our family, our work, our routine. But God created us to grow! Take on a new project at church. Become a hospice volunteer. Challenge yourself mentally or physically. Anything that stretches you, expands your world, or helps you share yourself with others will foster contentment and give you a fresh perspective on your life.

FIND PLACES OF PEACE

It's hard to open ourselves to the peace that passes understanding when we're constantly on the run. Part of contentment is a sort of spiritual sitting still that says, *I'm here and it is good and God is good.* So allow yourself the regular gift of listening to restful Christian music, taking a quiet walk by yourself, or stroking your pet.

We may never achieve absolute contentment. But as we seek God's peace and ask his help in setting our mind on "things above"—no matter what the world may be throwing at us—we may be able to say, echoing the apostle Paul, "I *am learning* to be content in every circumstance." Come to think of it, that would make a great inscription for a plaque. I could hang it in my kitchen and meditate on it as I start boiling the macaroni for dinner.

WHEN'S THE LAST TIME YOU TRULY LAUGHED—NOT ONE OF
those social polite laughs, but a real from-the-belly laugh? The
phrase "Laughter is good medicine" is true—laughter lightens
our·spirits, makes even hard tasks seem more manageable, and
changes our perspective.

If you need more laughter in your life, try these suggestions
by Carole Mayhall. Then practice at least one laugh a day.
You'll be amazed how you'll "lighten up"!

Laugh Every Day

CAROLE MAYHALL

God wants us to take serious things seriously—our life, the
Scriptures, sin—but he also encourages us to take upon
ourselves his "light" burden or, in a modern-day phrase, to
"lighten up" (see Matt. 11:28-30). God knows that pure,
uproarious, unself-conscious laughter can make us feel better not only emotionally but also physically!

If your ability to laugh has faded, here's how to develop
this incredible gift God's given us.

LOOK FOR HUMOR IN EVERYDAY HAPPENINGS

If there are children around—and you tune in—inevitably your
funny bone will be tickled. And when it is, allow yourself to
laugh aloud. Cultivate this habit, and it will change the way
you feel about yourself and the circumstances you're in.

Not long ago, as I waited for my husband, Jack, in the
customer-service area of a store, I began a conversation with
a precocious four-year-old boy. When he went to get a drink,
I asked him where the water went.

He pointed to his mouth and said, "In there."

"In your esophagus?" I pursued.

"No!" He laughed. "A 'sophagus is a spider animal."

"Oh? What does a 'sophagus look like?"

His eyes widened with delight. And off he went into the most imaginative and delightful description of a "'sophagus" you ever heard. Gone were my doldrums and impatience at having to wait in an uncomfortable chair.

EXPOSE YOURSELF TO FUNNY BOOKS, ARTICLES, TAPES, AND CARTOONS

When you find something that makes you laugh, clip it and save it to reread on a rough day. The more humor you expose yourself to, the easier it will become to look on the lighter side. You can also pass "cheer-germs" on if you're alert to things that would be funny to others. My daughter, Lynn, sends us cartoons, and we always get a laugh from them. Don't be timid about sharing something funny you've collected with a friend or relative who might need cheering up!

LOOK FOR PEOPLE WHO'VE MASTERED THE ART OF LAUGHTER AND CULTIVATE THEM AS FRIENDS

They'll build you up and help you learn to take life and its problems less seriously.

PRAY THAT GOD WILL DEEPEN YOUR CONVICTION THAT HE IS A GOD WHO SMILES

Carved in stone in California's Forest Lawn Cemetery are these words from the Founders' Creed: "Most of all I believe in a Christ who smiles and loves you and me."

Do you often picture Christ smiling? Can you possibly believe that the one who created the three-toed sloth, the platypus, and human beings *doesn't* have a giant sense of humor? Laughter reflects a significant spiritual truth—God delights in laughter and, most important, in us.

I'm awed every time I read Ephesians 1:11: "Moreover, because of what Christ has done, we have become gifts to God *that he delights in"* (TLB, emphasis added). Incredible! This truth alone should make us laugh aloud with joy.

DO YOU WORRY A LOT—AND WISH YOU COULD STOP worrying? If you really want to stop thinking the worst first, read what Scripture says. Habitual worry is at odds with faith in Christ—a faith that teaches us that "all things are possible with God" and to "cast our cares on him."

How can we break free from the worry that hampers us from living an abundant Christian life? The choice is ours. With the power of the Holy Spirit, we *can* transform our worry habits into ones that are pleasing to God. Here's how.

TRANSFORM NEGAHOLISM INTO HOPE
JANE JOHNSON STRUCK

 DISTANCE IS A GOOD THING   "When somebody is stuck in negativism, she really needs some objectivity, someone to tell her, 'Look, you're way out of line in your thinking,'" says Dr. Ray Mitsch, a clinical psychologist.

When an unexpected biopsy triggered overwhelming fear in my life, the calm, objective counsel and prayers of a close friend became invaluable. She was able to listen to my fears, then gently point out how my "end-of-the-world" scenarios were based on speculation, not evidence.

 WHAT'S YOUR MOTIVE?   "Ask yourself, What am I avoiding by being panicky, negative, or fearful?" says Sheri Klinka, program director for a Minirth-Meier clinic's day hospital and a licensed social worker. "Many times negative behavior becomes a way to avoid dealing with something the Holy Spirit may be convicting you to change."

Is your pessimism triggered by disappointment over relationships, anger with God, or fear of having to admit your own role in whatever problems you face? The sooner you own up to what lies behind the negaholism, the easier it becomes to develop a strategy for change.

COMPARE YOUR FEELINGS TO SCRIPTURE Lies about who God is and how he works can permeate our thoughts—and thoughts dictate our feelings. One woman told me that journaling helps her sort through her thoughts and align her emotions with biblical truths. "As I read back through it, I tell myself, *This is how I feel—now here is what the Bible says about the situation.*"

 SWITCH THE STATION We can make a conscious effort to reroute our thoughts, but it's God's Spirit that can "reprogram" our mind and heart. When I indulge myself in pessimism, it's time for me to steep myself in prayer. I've also found it comforting to memorize Scriptures that remind me of God's constant care and availability. When I allow these verses to settle deep within my heart, when I consciously dwell on these words and others, I have the ammunition I need to help keep my negative thoughts at bay.

 FACE YOUR FEARS HEAD-ON I once read the following observation: "Fear is the little darkroom where negatives are developed." One way to expose those negatives when they crop up unexpectedly is to offer them up to God in prayer. As Klinka says, "God never promised us the world would be a rosy place. But he has promised to be with us and equip us to deal with problems and tragedy. It's a spiritual battle: Is God sufficient or not? It comes back to the issue of trusting God."

 HAVE A "WHATEVER" FAITH God doesn't call us to blind optimism—to close our eyes and ignore the flaws around us, the dangers that exist, the consequences of a fallen world. But he does call us to what Klinka calls a "whatever" faith—trusting God *no matter what.* He wants us to be willing to see our health, our job, our relation-ships, our future, even the world around us, with a perspec-tive that mirrors his own.

"YOU SHOULD HAVE SEEN HER DRESS. IT WAS GHASTLY!"
"Listen to what Anne's kid just did. . . ." "You really should pray
for Tina. Did you know that . . . ?"

Gossip—those hot, juicy bits of information we love to hear
and spread. But, as the old saying goes, "What goes around
comes around." And if you've been on the receiving end of gossip, you know how painful and embarrassing it can be.

When you're tempted to gossip, watch what you say—and
spread "good gossip" instead! Here's how:

Spread "Good Gossip"
DANDI DALEY MACKALL

Each day we choose what information we'll take from conversations and repeat to others. Because kind, encouraging
words have a powerful potential to affect us for good, here's
how we can spread "good gossip"—by cultivating the habit
of passing along praise!

1. Check your vision. We all can find things to criticize:
"Somebody cut me off." "Nobody ever listens to my
ideas at work." "I always pick the wrong grocery line."
But how often do we notice the driver who let us enter
the freeway—or the waitress who gave us such great service?

The apostle Paul wrote the Philippians, "Whatever is true,
whatever is noble, whatever is right, whatever is pure, whatever is lovely, whatever is admirable—if anything is excel-
lent or praiseworthy—think about such things" (4:8). If we
want to build others up with "good gossip," we first need to
catch them being good!

2. Pass it on. Laurie's son Craig played junior high soccer,
and she was used to hearing from the coaches or other
mothers about how rambunctious Craig was. So when one

of the mothers who drove the boys told her, "Your son, Craig, is such a gentleman. Whenever he rode with us, he always thanked us and was so respectful," she was flabbergasted.

"You know," Laurie admits, "Craig hears from me every single time someone reports to me about how bad he is. But I need to go home right now and tell him about this good report!"

Whether it's sharing at a prayer meeting how an absent believer is walking in faith, or telling your daughter that her father mentioned to you how responsible she's becoming, praise is meant to be repeated. So take advantage of the tremendous opportunities to edify and encourage that all too often pass by unnoticed.

3. Put it in reverse. Once a piece of gossip begins to travel, it gains speed and becomes hard to stop. There's something horribly satisfying in seeing others knocked down, as if their descent in some way elevates us. It takes courage to reverse gossip. It may seem more fun to join in, more comfortable to keep quiet. But if we determine to pass along only the good, soon we'll be able to change the direction of the bad.

Elaine and her two sisters, Brenda and Nancy, have gone through their share of sibling rivalry over the years. "One day I was complaining to Brenda that Nancy never keeps in touch, that she's too caught up in her own life," says Elaine. "To my surprise, instead of seconding my criticism, Brenda replied, 'The last time I talked to Nancy, she told me she missed you. And she mentioned she's learned a lot about being a good mother just by watching you with your kids.' That comment stopped me in my tracks."

So when gossip is passed on to you, find a way to pass along a blessing in its place. Spread kind words—and let good news travel fast!

REMEMBER THOSE AWKWARD ADOLESCENT YEARS? THE
time you got your first bra and stuffed it so you weren't so
flat-chested at school? The party you wanted to go to just because
everybody else was going? The jeans you insisted your mom buy
because your best friend had that brand?

Peer pressure doesn't end with adolescence—it escalates.
We wonder, *Am I doing as much for my children as Karen
does? How come all my friends are getting married and I'm
not? Why am I the only one with an old, leaky refrigerator?*

Here's how to resist peer pressure.

RESIST PEER PRESSURE
JANIS LONG HARRIS

It's one thing to say it's important to live your life without
undue concern for what others think; it's another thing to
do it. Here are some tips I've found helpful:

💡 IT'S YOUR DECISION Decide to resist negative peer
pressure. "I'm making a conscious effort to care less about
what other people think and how they're rating me," says
Anne. "For instance, I ask myself, Am I getting angry at my
child because she's not meeting someone else's expectations or because she really needs to be disciplined?"

💡 NARROW YOUR CIRCLE OF APPROVAL While few of us are
impervious to the opinions of others, it's good to narrow
the circle of those whose approval you seek. Pam, an
at-home mother, says, "I focus on people I really admire.
There are so many people in my church, for example, who
are supportive of my staying at home to raise my children
that I try to think about them and not worry about the rest."

💡 THE GOOD, THE BAD, AND THE NEUTRAL Realize that peer
pressure isn't always bad. "I tend to set pretty easygoing
standards for myself, so peer pressure makes me shape

up—to get my degree, do more volunteer work, join a health club and exercise," admits my friend Kim.

When peer pressure is neither good nor bad, some women choose to conform rather than expend the effort to resist conformity. Diane, for example, is uncomfortable with the way her friends hug each other at church and social gatherings. She could tell them she's just not that demonstrative. But because she knows they're expressing genuine warmth and affection, she goes along with the custom.

 DON'T WORRY WHAT OTHERS THINK Learn the difference between Christian concern for the feelings of others and an unhealthy obsession with what others are thinking of you. "Some people think they're showing care for others' feelings when what they're really concerned about is conforming to others' expectations," points out pastoral counselor Bonnie Niswander. "To care about what others think and grow from it is different from worrying about what others think of you."

 PRAY, AND THEN PRAY AGAIN! Draw on your spiritual resources. "Prayer is one way I resist peer pressure," says Pam. "When I take my concerns to God, just the act of doing that releases me from a lot of concern about what others think."

 SEEK THE APPROVAL THAT COUNTS "So much of our mind-set is geared to seeking the approval of others," observes Julie. "Seeking God's approval doesn't come as naturally. But I'm finally coming to realize that happiness has to be related to doing what's right for God."

As a Christian, my goal is to become more sensitive to the right kind of pressure—the gentle promptings of the Lord who created me and offers me the strength I need to live a life that pleases him.

DO YOU WISH . . .

- you were more domestically talented, like your friend Susie?
- you knew God's purpose for your life?
- you knew what you were good at?

God is a unique Creator, and he has created each of us as *individuals*. This means that no one does things like you do—or is supposed to! If you sometimes think you're nothing special, think again. And then discover along with author Ruth Van Reken who God has created you to be!

Be You, Because That's How God Made You!

RUTH E. VAN REKEN

One day as I was asking God why he'd made me so ordinary, I picked up my Bible and read, "Don't cherish exaggerated ideas of yourself or your importance, but try to have a sane estimate of your capabilities" (Rom. 12:3, Phillips).

Are you kidding? I thought. *An exaggerated idea of myself is the least of my problems!*

But I did wonder, *What's a "sane estimate" of my capabilities? Do I have any? If so, what are they?*

Following are some basic principles God gave me for discovering who he made me to be. Living by them has done more for my low self-esteem than a thousand "how to" books.

WHEN GOD MADE YOU, HE MADE YOU RIGHT

My first mistake was comparing myself to everyone else. Comparisons usually result in discontent. God says he has a unique purpose for my life, and he created me with everything I need to fulfill it (Eph. 2:10). If I'm missing particular gifts—like artistic skills or organizational genius—I won't need them to accomplish what God has in mind for me.

LAY DOWN YOUR PLANS AND DREAMS

Before I could discover God's plans for me, I had to relinquish my own. In Romans 12:1, Paul tells us to give ourselves to God as a "living sacrifice."

Years ago I went all the way to Africa as a missionary nurse—but that wasn't the sacrifice. The hard part came when I realized God's plans for me differed markedly from my own.

The true celebrities are those who are victorious in situations where no one knows what they're doing but the Lord God.

BODIE THOENE

After all my schooling and resettling in a new country, my lifelong dream of having a magnificent medical ministry never even began. My three pre-schoolers needed help adjusting to our transcontinental move. And all day, every day, an unending stream of national children came to my kitchen door asking for cold water to drink. I couldn't get anything else done!

Anybody could pass out water, I reasoned. I wanted a *real* job. Yet God's ways are not my ways, and his thoughts are not my thoughts (Isa. 55:8). Finally, in faith, I laid down my dreams and took up his opportunities—ordinary, everyday cups of water.

MAKE A LIST OF WHAT DOES—AND DOESN'T— "COME NATURALLY"

Although I'd basically accepted God's decision to dispense water instead of medicine, some days I still wrestled until I read *Discovering Your Place in the Body of Christ* by Selwyn Hughes. He writes that when we operate in the area of our gifts and God-given talents, we have "maximum effectiveness and minimum weariness." When we work outside those areas, we have "minimum effectiveness and maximum weariness."

So I made two lists. My first column was headed "Things I like to do or that come easily for me." Above the second column I wrote, "Things I don't like to do or that are hard for me." No problem filling that second side.

"Craft projects. Decorating my house. Housekeeping. Administration. Organizing others. Singing solos." And many more.

The "easily" column remained blank. Only trivial, everyone-can-do-*that* things came to mind. "Talking. Thinking. Asking questions." Big deal. I looked for more things. "Journaling. Cooking. Welcoming unexpected guests." Still nothing distinctive. I looked for help in Romans 12 and got more depressed. None of the first gifts listed—preaching, teaching, administration—were mine. Finally Paul mentioned one more. "Let the man who feels sympathy for his fellows in distress help them cheerfully" (Rom. 12:8, Phillips).

Sympathy?! I'd always felt sympathy for others. Since my high school days, people came to me with their problems. But how could anything that ordinary be a gift? Yet there it lay among all the other gifts—equally identified as God given. Now what?

BEGIN TO USE YOUR GIFTS—NO MATTER HOW INSIGNIFICANT THEY SEEM

Paul tells the Romans not only to figure out their gifts but to concentrate on using them.

As I looked at my column of gifts, it dawned on me I'd already used many of these attributes. Friends laughingly dubbed our African home "Hotel Van Reken" for the steady stream of people flowing through it. But now I saw those people weren't unplanned interruptions in my schedule. Rather, they were God's assignments for me—and ones I could do at home while taking care of my kids! The lengthy conversations at my kitchen door, around meals, or late at night were ways God used my gift of sympathy through "talking, thinking, and asking questions" to comfort and encourage others. Writing in my journal gave me practice for writing follow-up letters as people moved away.

ASK GOD HOW YOU CAN SERVE HIM RIGHT NOW AND THEN DO IT

Three years later author and speaker Jill Briscoe came to our town. By then I'd begun using my gifts to lead a small Bible study. After one of Jill's seminars, I asked her, "How did you develop your groups into such a large network?"

Jill looked me in the eye and said, "Ruth, just ask God what's in front of your face and do it. Lots of people never do *anything* because they can't figure out how to do *everything*."

God has all the time in the universe. He's not bound by my to-do lists. God is also the Author of all things perfect—yet he loves me, warts and all.

JEANNE ZORNES

Powerful, practical, life-changing words. Ten years ago we moved back to the States, and I became an ordinary suburban housewife. No children at my kitchen door for water. I felt I was back to square one.

But by asking God, "What's in front of my face today?" I've learned to see his hand at work here as well. Thirsty children may be gone, but in this frenetic world, countless people suffer deep emotional and spiritual thirst. Phoning someone while I'm doing the dishes might be that person's cup of cold water. Listening and talking with a friend over lunch can be the perfect moment to remind each other of God's sovereignty and love.

CELEBRATE YOUR GOD-GIVEN GIFTS

Learning what I'm gifted in has led me to heartfelt yeses— and the liberating sense of finding my specific niche in God's kingdom. Learning what I'm not gifted in has led to wonderfully guilt-free nos (most days)! Best of all, I've learned when Jesus said he could give me an abundant life (John 10:10), he meant it. It's a lot more fun being who God made me instead of trying to be someone else!

TO-DO LISTS ARE SCATTERED THROUGH OUR DAYS: WORK schedules, freelance meetings, church commitments, volunteer work, carpooling. It seems each day the list grows bigger, and nothing ever gets taken off!

A year ago, after watching me frantically try to control my schedule, a wise friend told me to take a look at my daytimer. "Just by looking at it," she commented, "you can tell what's important to you—and who's in charge of your schedule."

Whose schedule are *you* following—yours or God's? This next story by Mayo Mathers will help you find out.

Live by God's Schedule

MAYO MATHERS

Late one night, I wearily pulled into a little motel after several hours of driving. Earlier that evening I'd been the guest speaker at a dinner meeting—the last of four out-of-state engagements. Afterwards, I'd decided to drive as fast as I could toward my home so I'd have a shorter drive the next day.

I was so tired I didn't even unload my suitcase from the car. I pulled out my nightgown and toothbrush, pushed open the motel door, and crashed on the bed. Before falling asleep, I called home to let my family know where I was.

"Mom!" urged my son, Landon, when he heard my voice. "You gotta get home early tomorrow! It's Homecoming and everyone's coming here for dinner before the game. They want you to fix lasagna!" I assured him I'd be home in plenty of time. Then, before hanging up, my husband reminded me I also had billing to do for our business. *How am I ever going to get everything done tomorrow?* I wondered. My last thought before going to sleep was a question: *God, have I misunderstood your will in my life?*

When I first began speaking to women's groups, I had no

doubt this was a ministry God had given me, and I happily accepted every invitation I received. At first, most were from nearby towns, but soon they poured in from locations that required me to be gone for several days. It was becoming impossible to balance my family, ministry, and other commitments. None were getting the attention they deserved.

Driving home the next morning, I prayed as I sorted through my thoughts. Then I remembered Psalm 90:12: "Teach us to number our days and recognize how few they are; help us to spend them as we should" (TLB). *Was I really doing that?*

Over the next several weeks, I began to see that just because some outside commitments were worthwhile didn't mean they were God's will for *me*. A friend once told me, "There are many good things a Christian can do, but only do what God shows you is best." I realized the only way to do that is to begin each day by relinquishing its hours to God and letting *him* establish the balance between my marriage, family, career, and ministry.

Just this week I received an invitation to speak at an evangelistic seminar in a city I've wanted to visit. And the topic was an exciting one I'd been researching. Thinking of the opportunity it would provide to share Christ, I eagerly reached for my calendar, despite the fact I already was committed to another out-of-state speaking engagement that month. Then God gave me a gentle nudge. *Whose schedule are you fitting it into?* he asked. *Mine or yours?* Putting my calendar away, I declined the invitation.

It's your schedule, God. Teach me to number my days.

THINK IT OVER
How's your "self" life? Do you need to be more involved with others, or less involved? Are you growing in contentment, happy with who you're becoming, or do you often feel overwhelmed and discontent? Take time to evaluate your self life honestly before God. And then ask him to give you the courage to make the needed changes.

Single Life

I'd love to come home to a husband—to share heartfelt thoughts with someone who utterly loves me and prays for me! And because God created us with physical desires, I long for physical intimacy—to be held and to become one with a man. But when I'm honest with God about my longing for marriage, an earthly home, and motherhood, God reminds me that, as his child, I'm a whole person—with or without a man.

KATHY TROCCOLI

How Do You Rate Your Single Life?

Single Life. We love it; we hate it. As singles, we have freedom to travel, to explore, to be spontaneous in our activities. But at the same time, we may return to a too quiet house, spend more alone time than we really want, and wish for consistent friends in our life.

And then there's the ever present specter of "dating" and all the questions associated with trying to find "Mr. Right" in a sinful universe: What qualities should I look for? How do I know if he really loves me—or I love him? When should I break off a relationship? Does God have a "special someone" planned for me or not? And, if so, how and when will I find that man?

These questions, and more, can lead to tremendous confusion and frustration in what seems to be a "couple-centered" world. At times we may even wonder where God is, in the "dailies" of our life alone. But God has promised never to leave us or forsake us.

We can learn to be content and balanced in this area of our life, too—even if we aren't "happy" about not being married. This chapter will help you appreciate your single state and anticipate all the wonderful future plans God has for you!

"I HAVE A TOUGH TIME BEING ALONE AFTER WORK," MY friend Shellie admitted. "I think of my friends who are married, who go home to their husbands and have someone to talk to. But at the same time, I don't have to rush around getting dinner ready because it's just me. I can just relax—and eat whenever I wish!"

In every stage of life there are positives and negatives. As we learn to focus on the positives, the negatives no longer seem so difficult. What's to celebrate about being single? Read on—and you'll see!

Celebrate Being Single!

S U S A N   C O K E R

I never envisioned being thirtysomething and single. When I was growing up, every adult woman I knew was married—as well as most of the female characters in movies and on television. The fairy tales my mother read to me always ended with "and *they* lived happily ever after." Like most little girls, I dreamed of the day my prince would come and we would ride off *together*.

Then age twenty-four came and went, with no change in my marital status. I broke up with my college boyfriend and took a job as a publicist. Family trauma struck—both my father and grandmother died of cancer. I discovered an inner reservoir of strength as I dealt with these losses. And for the first time I realized that God had a personal interest in my welfare. Other people might come and go in my life, but God would always be there for me.

However, at the same time, I was profoundly angry. I felt God had let me down. Why did he allow people I loved to die? Why couldn't I have someone to lean on, to take care of me—a flesh-and-blood someone who'd never say good-bye?

I began a precarious balancing act between utter dependence on God and the certainty I'd never make it without another human being beside me. Ten years later the pendulum continues to swing between these extremes, stopping at various points on a given day. I wish I could say I've found complete contentment living life on my own. But I haven't.

I'm not one of those people the apostle Paul spoke about who possess the gift of singleness. But I do agree with Paul that we're supposed to learn to be content, no matter what the circumstance. And I've found the process is easier if I give myself to the things that matter most. It's then I've discovered some positive aspects to being single.

People tell us sex is OK, that you can do whatever you want, that loving someone is all that matters. Even if it seems right, God's Word says it's not. He designed one man for one woman for all time. I believe if we set our heart on the Lord and covenant with him to be pure, he will honor that. And the rewards of obedience are great.

KIM HILL

DEVELOPING CLOSE FRIENDSHIPS WITH WOMEN

My singleness has provided opportunities to experience the friendship and support of other women. A year ago I started a prayer group in my home. Every Tuesday night four of us (all single women) meet to discuss what's going on in our life and to pray together. As one friend put it, "There've been many weeks when I've thought, *I can make it . . . if I can just make it till Tuesday."* I'm grateful for these Christian friends who've been extensions of God's grace to me.

GETTING TO KNOW YOURSELF

With a husband and two sons, my sister, Laura, has little time for herself. But as a single, I've been freer to explore who I am. I've been able to curl up with hundreds of good books, visit art museums, and watch dozens of sappy romantic movies. I've traveled to many interesting places and taken last-minute vacations to the beach when I needed a breather, without coordinating my life around anyone else's schedule. I've had the free time to take courses in a variety of subjects that interest me, such as photography and creative writing. All of this has helped me tap into parts of myself I might never have discovered had I married at a young age.

GIVING TO OTHERS

Singleness offers a unique opportunity to give our time and talents to others. I once spent the holiday season organizing my city's "Angel Tree" program, a ministry of Prison Fellowship that provides gifts to children of prisoners. Rather than give in to the loneliness that often hits at Christmas, I decided to spend my time making someone else's holiday a little brighter.

EXPLORING YOUR CAREER

While I'm humbled by the working wives and mothers I know who literally work from dawn until dusk to meet the many obligations of home and career, I don't envy them. It looks like awfully hard work!

I'm grateful I've been able to carve a career for myself in the demanding profession of public relations without sacrificing home and family in the process. If I have to work overtime, I don't have to worry that my family is waiting for dinner. When I come home exhausted, I can collapse on the couch or relax in a bubble bath. Because my job requires a lot of travel, I can go anywhere at a moment's notice without feeling guilty about not giving enough quality time to my family.

ENJOYING YOUR FREEDOM

All the single and married women I talked with mentioned "financial, personal, and professional freedom" when listing the positive aspects of being single. One single friend was able to move across the country without a job waiting for her because she felt God's leading and wanted to live in another city. "If I'd been married and had a family, I'm not sure I'd have been able to do that," she says.

TRUSTING IN GOD

My single friend, Heather, recently left her full-time job as a magazine editor to pursue a freelance writing career. She enjoys her newfound freedom and can't imagine going back to the tedious routine of a nine-to-five job. But, without the support of a regular paycheck, she's had to learn to trust God for her *every* need—from daily meals to office equipment.

Of this I'm certain— whatever my marital status, true joy comes only from total surrender to Christ.
PEGGY BRAMBLETT

Directly experiencing God's provision is one of the greatest benefits of being single. It still amazes me that he cares for all my needs. When I pray, "Give us this day our daily bread," I know God will answer. And when he does, I've no one to thank except him.

EXPERIENCING A DEEPER RELATIONSHIP WITH JESUS

If we're completely honest, most of us single women never outgrow our desire for a husband and family. But it's dangerous to expect a spouse or family member to totally fulfill us. My friend Beth observes, "If all our longings were taken away, would we really go to God?"

As single women, we can experience great joy and peace if we allow Jesus the place in our heart we've been saving for that special man. That means spending time with Jesus regularly, talking things over with him in prayer as if he were our closest companion (which, of course, he is), and doing our best to place his desires for our life over our own.

We all have longings that won't be fulfilled this side of heaven, longings so deep we can't even verbalize them. But Jesus knows what we long for, and because he understands, he comforts us along the way.

ALONE TIME. WE ALL NEED IT. TIME ALONE GIVES US THE
chance to breathe a sigh of relief, to do something we've been
longing to do, to get away from all the busy activity of the
world. Some of us crave alone time; others run from it, because
it would mean facing fears we don't want to face, such as
Won't I ever get married? and *Why am I so cautious about
getting to know others?*

Here's why alone time is so important—and why you
should schedule some for yourself:

Use Alone Time to Refuel

JUDITH COUCHMAN

You're seated in a theater and notice a woman alone in the
next row. Do you pity or admire her? Your response reveals
your attitude about being alone.

If you think she's lonely or unable to scrounge a date, it's
time to reconsider your opinions, even face fears. Keeping
company with yourself doesn't mean you're a hermit or—
worse yet—socially unacceptable. Even Jesus went away
from his disciples and the crowds continually surrounding
him to take a break, to have some "alone time."

Whether you have too much alone time or not enough, it's
time to strike a balance. Being alone doesn't mean lonely;
alone time can be delightful. It means:

1. A time to refuel. A demanding job, children underfoot,
an apartment of roommates, carpooling to and from day
care, church and community involvements: No matter how
wonderful, commitments drain your energy. Private time
replenishes inner resources so you can fulfill them.

You may require total solitude. Or, like the woman at the
theater, an outing by yourself. Attending an event alone
doesn't mean you're a social misfit. It indicates inner security.

2. A time to rest. Take a vacation without leaving home. Browse through magazines, indulge in a favorite food, play soft music, and pretend you're at the beach.

Declare yourself off-limits to people and phone calls, even if it's just for an hour. The mind and body need periodic rest.

You're not a bad friend, mother, sister, or employee for taking alone time. Friends and family will appreciate a rejuvenated you.

3. A time to grow. Read a book, listen to lecture tapes, pursue a mind-stretching hobby, or write about your feelings. These activities stimulate you intellectually. And they require time alone.

4. A time to catch up. If your kids are gone with your ex for the evening, or you have a free Saturday afternoon with no commitments, you can use alone time to catch up on business, letter writing, organizing your home, or anything nagging for your attention (laundry, writing birthday cards, and wrapping gifts, etc.). Even a few hours can provide a wonderful sense of accomplishment. So determine not to waste them with procrastination, too much television, napping, daydreaming at length, or stretching small tasks into all-consuming projects.

5. A time for God. A personal relationship requires one-to-one time. Don't ignore getting alone with Christ and practicing the basics: confessing your sins, reading and memorizing Scripture, praying about people or problems, and thanking God for his goodness.

If your mind wanders, use a Bible study guide for structure. Developing your soul is as important as nurturing your family and friends.

Remember: Different people need varying amounts of alone time. So create private time to uniquely fit you—your needs and personality.

"WHEN MY BEST FRIEND, LISA, GOT MARRIED," MY FRIEND
Alice complained, "she disappeared from my life. I'd call, and she
never had time to go out. Now, a year later, she's started to
pursue me. I just don't get it."

She's not the only one. It's tough when a friend gets married. Up to that point, all her friends have been "her universe."
Then marriage hits, and her universe widens to include another
person and his family and friends.

All friendships require communication and flexibility, and
single/married friendships are no exception. But with a little fine-
tuning, they're worth it. Here's how:

FINE-TUNE RELATIONSHIPS WITH MARRIED FRIENDS
VINITA HAMPTON WRIGHT

The year after I graduated from high school, both of my best
friends got married. Both had a baby within the year. And both
seemed to forget I existed. One of the sources of sharpest pain
and conflict in friendship is the change that occurs when a
friend gets married. But it *is* possible to fine-tune your friendship
so it thrives throughout the seasons of life. Here are some tips to
take to heart if you're single:

 ACCEPT THE CHANGES Especially during the first year,
when your friend and her new husband are solidifying
their marriage, she may neglect other relationships. But
after a while she will come back to more balance, because
she still needs her other friends. And of course, she'll make
new friends who are also married. This isn't a rejection of
single friends but a recognition that she needs feedback
from women who have marital experience.

 BECOME A GOOD LISTENER Since marriage is the central
event of your friend's life, she'll talk about it—sometimes
more than you want to listen. Keep in mind she's
discovering a new identity and needs to work through it by

verbalizing it—especially to the very friends (like you!) who have helped her work through so many events in her life.

💡 REALIZE KIDS ARE PART OF GOD'S SCHEME If and when your friend becomes a mother, her life will revolve around that new human being for whom she is responsible. But she'll need your companionship more than ever; you may be one of the few adults she sees for days on end. Remember that children are part of God's scheme—you'll be amazed at the richness your friends' children can add to your life.

💡 GIVE THEM SPACE Regardless of how close your friendship was before her marriage, don't pop in anytime you need to process something going on in your own life. Healthy friendships have an equal exchange and incorporate some distance.

💡 INVITE HER OUT Don't assume your married friend will just want to be with married people or that she'll always insist on bringing her husband or the children. Invite her to the women's retreat. Take advantage of the times her husband is away to do something you both enjoy.

💡 SHARE YOUR STRUGGLES Most single adults experience periods of depression and/or anger at being alone. You may look at all your friends who have married and struggle with jealousy and self-doubt. *What's so wrong with me that I'm still alone?* Sometimes you begin to resent your friend for having what you want. It's OK to share your struggles with married friends, but don't heap guilt on them.

💡 APPRECIATE HER HUSBAND When a girlfriend marries, you've gained a potential brother and friend. Find ways of showing him Christlike love and acceptance (no matter how you feel about him). A wisely handled relationship with a friend's spouse can enrich your life and provide a safe place for you to learn more about relating to men.

AS SINGLES, WHAT WE DO, OUR WORK, IS A BIG AND
important part of our life. And that's as God intended it to be. But
for some of us, work crosses the line of becoming not only what
we *do,* but who we *are.* If you tend to chronically overwork, here
are some things to think about from Type-A-personality author
and speaker Elaine K. McEwan-Adkins.

Don't Overwork
ELAINE K. MCEWAN-ADKINS

Do you ever work late just to avoid going home to an empty
apartment? Do you find yourself being drawn into too many
projects so that you're overbusy? Do you say yes to a lot of
activities because you'd feel guilty if you said no? After all,
as a single you're "supposed" to have more time than married people because you have fewer family responsiblities.

But sometimes when we're single, we don't realize we
need special time for ourselves. We permit others to set our
agenda, feeling we have no right to be "selfish" with our
time or energies. We take on one more church activity,
feeling compelled to teach Sunday school even if it isn't our
gift. We find ourselves organizing all get-togethers with
friends, just because we, as singles, think we should. Why?
Because, of course, as singles, everyone knows we have
more time. Even employers and coworkers can subtly send
the message that since we don't have home responsibilities,
we're the perfect person to take on traveling or extra assignments at work (especially evening and weekend duty). You
may even be guilty of doing this to yourself. I know I was.

I was single for several years after my first husband died.
Eager to avoid spending an evening alone, I volunteered to
be the representative at a meeting no one else could attend.
I stayed late at the office and completed the report, while

everyone else working on it went home to family. Before I knew it, work consumed my life.

How do you know if you're too busy? Here's a quick list:

■ You wake up in the middle of the night to add more items to your "to do" list.

■ You don't have time to celebrate your own birthday.

■ You break down in tears for no apparent reason.

■ You forget to send a sympathy card to a friend.

■ You haven't eaten a meal that's not on the run for two weeks.

■ You read your mail and put on your makeup while you're driving to work.

■ You've lost your car keys three times in the last few days.

■ Your clean underwear has been in the dryer for a week.

■ You haven't read a good book in months.

If you've fallen into any of the above unhealthy traps, set about bringing balance to your life. Take charge of your calendar. Each week, schedule recreation, worship, social events, housecleaning, personal care, and shopping. When someone at the office asks you to do something extra, consult your calendar. If you've penciled in housecleaning or shopping, you have another commitment and can legitimately decline without apology or embarrassment.

Always remember that it's OK to just say no!

IN THE COURSE OF A NORMAL DAY, WE COLLECT SOME
bruises. We hear a harsh word, work too long, make a mistake,
deal with chaos, lose something important, or carry someone
else's burdens.

Multiply a day's bruises by 7, 30, or 365, and you'll discover a genuine need for some tender loving care. Although
you often receive comfort and encouragement from others, you
can't always wait for someone else to come to your aid. If you
need some TLC, give it to yourself! Here's how:

TAKE A BREAK—AND PAMPER YOURSELF
VINITA HAMPTON WRIGHT

> Sometimes the only person who can really care for you is
> *you.* So if you're feeling a bit battered these days, here are
> some tips to nurse yourself back to a healthier life:
>
> 💡 DARE TO DREAM Take an afternoon to write down all the
> crazy things you'd like to do. Don't worry about how
> plausible they may be or even if they are spiritual. Dream
> of places you'd like to see, projects you'd like to
> accomplish, the home you'd like to live in. Dream of
> ministry opportunities, personal growth, and blessings for
> family members. Many of life's positive changes start with
> a dream.
>
> 💡 TAKE A SEAT There's probably some place you especially
> enjoy—a forest preserve, park, coffee shop, library,
> bookstore, mall. You like the atmosphere, the food, the
> people. So go there—and pick a seat where you'll feel
> comfortable enough to write in your journal, read a
> magazine, do some needlework, or just watch the world
> go by.
>
> 💡 SLEEP ON IT If you're tired a lot, you may be stressed or
> depressed—or you simply may need some more sleep!

Take an afternoon nap. Try to sleep a full eight hours three nights in a row. Or stay in bed on a day when you have no appointments.

💡 RELISH YOUR OWN GIFTS God doesn't give you gifts just so you can bless others. Your ability to create recipes, write eloquently, play an instrument, paint, sculpt, sing, or sew is meant for your own nurture, too. Give yourself time not only to create anew but also to enjoy what you've produced in the past.

💡 BE GOOD TO YOUR BODY What makes you feel invigorated or rested? A long bath, a day or afternoon at a spa, a professional massage? A new haircut or perhaps a day of fasting? Indulge yourself for your body's sake. And we all know the benefits of exercise—the important thing is to do something you actually enjoy. Even a little exercise, especially if done regularly, is better than none at all.

💡 HAVE A GOOD LAUGH—OR CRY Allow yourself some privacy from time to time to feel what's going on inside you—joy, sadness, loneliness, excitement, anxiety, etc. Respond honestly before God to those emotions—and if you feel like crying, go ahead and cry.

💡 ENJOY GOD'S CREATURES Have you ever considered owning a pet, if you don't already? The right companion from the animal kingdom can have a calming effect on your jangled nerves. If a pet's out of the question, visit a zoo, pop into a pet shop, or view a nature video. Go outside and watch a squirrel travel from tree to tree or a bird search out breakfast in the grass.

💡 REVISIT A FAVORITE THING We all have special items that, for one reason or another, have the power to encourage and uplift us—a painting you're drawn to, a photo that always makes you smile, a well-loved book that reminds you of home. Take advantage of them.

DATING IS COMPLICATED—AND MESSY. ALL THAT SCOPING out, asking out, going out, evaluating, and maybe breaking up, only to start the cycle over is exhausting. So if you're not dating anyone right now, be thankful! When you feel discouraged about your single life, read this story by Taylor Jones. It'll change your perspective *and* give you a laugh!

Realize Being Alone on Valentine's Day Isn't All That Bad

TAYLOR JONES

As I stood in a grocery store checkout line at 9:30 P.M. last February 13, it suddenly struck me: *There's only one thing worse than not having a boyfriend on Valentine's Day— actually having one!*

You see, single women without a romantic interest on this day of love are only miserable for *one* flowerless day (a misery usually conquered by large quantities of after-holiday half-price Valentine's Day candy). But when you do have someone special in your life, you have a sleep-depriving, nail-biting decision (with relationship-making or -breaking ramifications) ahead: what to give this semi-significant other.

For single people, it's not just buying a gift, it's making a statement. For example, if a guy simply buys me a card, I know we're doomed. If he buys me a diamond necklace, I'm mentally picking out our china pattern. In some ways holidays provide a rare glimpse into the status of a relationship— information I usually have to pry out of my current flame in a slow and sometimes painful process.

Unfortunately, the stress of selecting a Valentine's Day gift is lopsided. Men have it easy: If they give any form of chocolate, they're right up there with Mel Gibson or "Superman" Dean Cain. A guy could give me chocolate in the shape of a station wagon (life-size, preferably), and I'd swoon at his romantic display. Then there's the whole "language of flowers" thing. Guys have it literally spelled out for them. A red rose means "I love you." A yellow rose communicates friendship. It couldn't get much easier.

But where is the male equivalent to flower language? Does the latest CD from his favorite group say "You're sweet"? Or does a power saw say "I'm crazy about you"? Without a universally recognized gift-giving language, a woman's left to second-guess what signals she's sending . . . and he's receiving.

It's all the symbolism and sentiment wrapped up in Valentine's Day gifts that often create so much stress. I learned this the hard way last year when I bought a pair of boxer shorts with glow-in-the-dark hearts on them for the guy I was dating at the time. He'd told me he collected funny boxers, and I thought these were too funny to pass up.

The media tells us that romance and sex are what count, not relationship. But what we really need is Jesus' love and a relationship with him. Only then can our deepest needs be satisfied.

FRANCINE RIVERS

But when I casually mentioned my gift to my coworkers— good Christian friends—on Valentine's Day eve, they responded with raised eyebrows. "But that's *underwear*," they informed me, explaining that my gift had a meaning they didn't want to get into and they hoped I wasn't trying to convey.

The last thing I wanted to do was communicate something suggestive, so I thanked my friends for their intervention, decided to stuff the boxers in the back of a drawer as soon as I got home so no one else would be privy to my near-miss romantic faux pas, and escaped to my office to panic. Unfortunately, I had an after-work commitment that tied me up until 9 P.M., so with no real time left for shopping, I was desperate.

That evening I rushed to the only place open after nine—

the grocery store. I was ashamed to be making what was no longer a thoughtful, romantic purchase—until I realized I wasn't alone. Stuffed into the card aisle, the candy section, and the floral department were half the men in the greater Chicago area! Under normal circumstances, this would've been a single woman's dream come true. But I had other things on my mind: *What on earth could I possibly buy my boyfriend in a grocery store?*

That's when I did it: I came up with the cheesiest gift in the history of Valentine's Day. I could almost feel Cupid wincing as I roamed from aisle to aisle gathering my gift of *red food*. Strawberries, spaghetti and spaghetti sauce, cherry Kool-Aid, strawberry Pop Tarts, picante sauce and chips, apples. *What bachelor doesn't need and want more food?* I reasoned—all the while knowing this was one of my dorkiest moves yet. *No wonder I'm still single,* I thought. If the boxer shorts would've given the wrong message, what did red food communicate? I didn't want to think about it.

Next, I elbowed my way into the dreaded greeting-card aisle. I can't count the number of cards I've read over the years searching for one appropriate for my current dating situation. In all honesty, I guess I shouldn't expect to see categories like "Guys you've broken up with and gotten back together with three times and you're still not sure how you stand," next to "Husband" and "Parents" in the card aisle. If I can't figure out a relationship, how can I expect Hallmark to?

So I stood there, reading card after card, thinking, *Too mushy, too racy, too cutesy, too romantic, too old-fashioned,* until I found the perfect one with an artistic-looking heart on the front and a blank inside. Once I got home, I penned my affections, wrapped the food in a big red box, and went to bed, fearing the imminent demise of our relationship.

The next day at work, Valentine's Day, the same coworkers inquired about Plan B. When I told them what I'd bought, they smiled politely. "How, um, practical," one woman said reassuringly. I closed my office door to conduct my panic in private.

Several hours later, after my boyfriend took me out for a nice lunch, the moment of truth arrived. We sat in the parking lot of my office building and exchanged gifts. When he handed me a familiar-looking rectangular box, my heart started racing. I opened the box, and the wonderful smell of chocolate filled his truck. I gave him a big hug of thanks.

Many people conveniently forget that there are more Christian women than Christian men. Not everyone is going to be able to pair up. But I've never seen the Scripture where God thinks less of a woman because she's not married. The truth is, God is a loving God, and he doesn't punish women by keeping them single.

MARGARET BECKER

Then, with a sheepish grin, I handed him my gift. He smiled at the warm words of my card, then tore open the box and peered in at the odd assortment of edibles. "Cool!" he said with an enthusiastic smile. He actually liked it!

I sat there dumbfounded as he happily sank his teeth into one of the apples. Suddenly it occurred to me that he was just as happy with the chips and salsa as he would have been with a shirt I'd have spent six hours in a mall picking out! I guess love really is a mystery.

Despite my creative approach to the challenging art of gift buying, we broke up several months later. As I approach this Valentine's Day alone, I may gaze longingly at the boxed chocolates and beautiful bouquets my friends and coworkers will receive, but I won't complain. In fact, one thought keeps coming to my mind: *What a relief!*

WHAT DO YOUR PRAYERS SOUND LIKE?

When I'm honest with myself, I realize that often I treat God as a vending machine who, if I pray hard enough, will dispense whatever I want into my eager hands. But because God knows what's best for us, many times his answer is "No," or "Wait." And, with my human shortsightedness, that can be pretty hard to take!

I've found, though, that when I leave my request and the situation in God's hands, he gives me peace—and he often surprises me with his answer! When author and speaker Liz Curtis Higgs began to pray God's way, here's what she learned:

Pray God's Way

LIZ CURTIS HIGGS

When my life calendar flipped over to thirty and I was still single, my prayers for a partner increased in intensity. "I'm lonely, Lord," I'd moan. "I want children. *Do* something!" His answer arrived, not in the form of a person but a verse: "Your Maker is your husband—the Lord Almighty is his name" (Isa. 54:5). Hanging onto that verse like a lifeline, I was delighted when someone who assumed I was married asked, "What does your husband do?" I smiled broadly and replied, "He runs the universe!"

Five years into my Christian life, I finally accepted God's response to my cry for companionship: "I love you, Liz, and I am enough." Then Bill stepped into my life. What my husband-to-be found was a woman focused on God, not on finding a man.

Little did I know I would pray that prayer again three years into our marriage: "I'm lonely, Lord! Send somebody!" Oh, life with Bill was wonderful—when we were together. But when he went to work for ten hours a day and I was home with a toddler and an infant, my heart longed for company that didn't require a diaper change. The heavenly response again: "I am enough, Liz."

Seeking his strength by filling the hours with his Word, I soon found myself leading a Bible study. In that small-group setting, some very special friendships with other at-home mothers developed. I'm a slow learner, but this lesson was abundantly clear: When I sought the Lord and looked outward to the needs of others, my own desires were met, too.

What we often forget is that God is with us in the loneliness, in the pain. He says, "I am with you. I've been here, and I am here." He doesn't necessarily take the pain itself away, yet he enables us to endure it because we are not suffering alone.

We know the Lord loves to hear the prayers of his children and wants us to "pray without ceasing." But prayer without seeking, knocking, and finding his will for us ultimately frustrates us and leaves us wondering, *Doesn't God care?* He cares very much—but more for our heart than our wish list.

God isn't Santa—he's Savior. He saves us not only from death but from ourselves and our foolish, selfish desires. Thankfully, God listens to his children, no matter how me-centered our prayers may be. The little sign in my office that says Prayer Changes Things has taken on a new meaning these days as I'm learning what prayer really changes—me!

THINK IT OVER
How do you feel about being single? Are you happy? angry? discouraged? not sure? Ask God to help you be content with your life. Turn to him in confidence, knowing that he, and he only, knows what the future holds and is working out his best for you.

Spiritual Life

As the years have passed, I'm totally
convinced the most valuable pursuit I embarked
on was that of knowing God.

KAY ARTHUR

ARE YOU GROWING SPIRITUALLY?

DO YOU EVER WONDER

- if God really loves you?
- if he's given you any talents—and if so, what they are?
- if he cares about your daily problems?
- if you can trust his promises?
- if he'll ever use you to impact someone else's life, for him?
- if he's truly listening to your prayers?

All of us long to be intimate with God and grow in our walk with him. We want strong relationships with family, friends, and the body of Christ—all by-products of a strong spiritual life. But, let's face it—sometimes we just feel stagnant in our spiritual growth. We're often frustrated in growing closer to God because of interruptions and personal crises, difficult relationships, busyness, and even lack of discipline.

Is it possible to grow spiritually in spite of these daily hindrances? Yes, for God promised us that "if . . . you seek the Lord your God, you will find him if you look for him with all your heart and with all your soul" (Deut. 4:29). This chapter will show you how.

SEVENTEEN YEARS AGO I PRAYED A DANGEROUS PRAYER. Because I was an on-the-go person, the most hated word in my vocabulary was *wait*. So after some prodding from a friend, I asked God to give me more patience. What did God do? He brought circumstances into my life during the next few years (and still is!) to accomplish what I asked for!

Exciting things happen when you pray. So if you're bored with your prayer life and wonder if God is really listening, try these dangerous prayers of pastor Bill Hybels.

Pray Dangerously

BILL HYBELS

"Dear Lord, get me through today," Laura prayed silently as she drove to work. "Please watch over my family. Help me complete everything I need to do today."

Do you pray a quick prayer each morning—like Laura—for your family's safety as you travel to the office? Or do you recite a prayer before your breakfast or dinner? Do you tenderly tuck in your kids after you join in their bedtime prayers or pray a long conversational prayer during your morning devotions?

Each day we pray all kinds of prayers—from the safe or self-serving to the risky and exciting. When was the last time you prayed a "dangerous" prayer—a prayer that put your faith on the line and opened you up to God in a way you've never done before?

God loves to hear dangerous prayers—the kind of prayers that help us grow as Christians. Scripture is riddled with the prayers of believers who wanted to mature in their Christian walk. If you have been keeping God at a safe distance in your prayer life, try praying one of the following "dangerous" prayers—and see how God in his wisdom will answer it:

SEARCH ME

How easy it is for us to feel righteous indignation at people who rebel against God—and forget to ask God first if there is any rebellion in *us*. David the psalmist realized he needed to pray a "search me" prayer—and before we start getting agitated at the sins of others, we need to pray this as well: "Search me, O God, and know my heart; test me and know my anxious thoughts. See if there is any offensive way in me, and lead me in the way everlasting" (Ps. 139:23-24).

Prayer is cooperation with God: not getting what I want but learning what he wants.

ELISABETH ELLIOT GREN

There's an old adage that says, "Don't ask the question if you're not ready to hear the answer." A "search me" prayer is dangerous because when you ask God to search your heart for anything that hurts or displeases him, he will. The Holy Spirit exposes those closed-off areas in your life that need to be changed, and you can't plead ignorance anymore. Don't pray a "search me" prayer unless you're ready for that kind of exposure. Seriously committed believers pray "search me" prayers to eliminate the sin in their lives and help them mature in their Christian walk.

BREAK ME

"I just can't seem to stop trying to impress everyone I meet," a woman admitted to me recently. "I guess I worry too much about what they'll think of me. I'm afraid I'll be rejected if I don't measure up. So I constantly end up in a vicious cycle of worry and fear!"

Ecclesiastes 3:3 says that there's "a time to tear down and a time to build." If you are ever going to grow as a Christian, you need to pray a "break me" prayer. No matter where you are spiritually, there's always some area in which you need God's intervention. Maybe you need to tear down the pattern of perfectionism or too much concern over your reputation, like the woman just mentioned. Or maybe you struggle with fear, lust, greed, or jealousy.

As we mature as believers, new Christlike patterns need to replace the old. God is the only one who has the power to help us overcome the old patterns. So if you want to be set free to follow Christ fully, then it's time to pray a "break me" prayer.

STRETCH ME

Cindy is caught in a difficult marriage to a man who doesn't share her Christian values and doesn't meet many of her emotional needs.

"At first I was always asking God to change my husband, change my circumstances, make everything perfect the way I'd like it to be," she admits. "But now I've come to realize that instead of letting me escape my problems, God wants me to grow through them—he wants to stretch my faith."

"Stretch me" prayers are the kind you pray when you want to grow up spiritually. In the early days of the church, believers were routinely beaten, jailed, and later fed to lions in the Colosseum. But instead of praying, "God, take away the persecution," believers prayed, "Stretch our courage, stretch our boldness!" As a result, the early church grew, both spiritually and numerically, in the face of tremendous opposition.

You may not face the kind of physical opposition the early church did, but perhaps you feel stuck, tired of going nowhere spiritually or relationally. Is your marriage difficult like Cindy's? Are your children going through tough times and you're not sure how to cope? Ask God to stretch your marriage, your parenting, your spiritual understanding, even your courage to walk with him in a new way.

If you've ever met a woman whose depth of love humbled you, whose perseverance inspired you, whose patience challenged you, or whose strength amazed you, you probably met a woman who prayed a "stretch me" prayer. Such strengths of character are won only by those who respond to life's challenges by asking God to stretch them.

LEAD ME

When you get settled into a house, a career, a growing family, or future plans, it's tempting to avoid dangerous "lead me" prayers that may "unsettle" your life such as, "God, take my whole life, and do what you want." It's scary to open yourself to God's control. But that's where faith comes in. We need to believe God loves us and wants to lead our life down a better, more exciting path than we could ever lead ourselves.

When you say, "God, here's my life. I'll follow your promptings, I'll listen for the tugs of your Spirit"—you'll be surprised to see what can happen.

While you're suffering, you can't see the why. It's only after the fact that you see God makes true his promises—he works all things together for good.

JAN DRAVECKY

USE ME

A "use me" prayer says, "God, I'm available if you'd like to do something great through me. I'm available if you'd like to touch another life through me."

"Use me" prayers are powerful. They create adventures. You never know what the result of these prayers will be, but they're worth the risk of praying, because when you ask God to use you, he will. And it's wonderful to be used by God. Praying these five dangerous prayers says you mean business with God. When you prayerfully and courageously move out of your comfort zone, your spiritual life will never be the same.

MANY WOMEN THINK THAT IN ORDER FOR GOD TO USE them, they must be part of an organized ministry, have a traumatic background or gripping testimony, or be specially talented. Not true. The good news is that God can use you—in whatever situation you are in today—to make a difference in others' lives. And whether your personal ministry impacts many people or just a few, you'll find that giving back to God also makes a difference in *you*. Here's how to find your niche of ministry:

Find Your Ministry Niche

MARITA LITTAUER

As you look at your own life experiences and resources, you may have an idea of what you could do to give back to others. But how can you tell if your ideas are God's plan for your personal ministry? Here are some steps to guide you to your ministry niche:

1. Know God. If we want to hear God's voice, we first need to know him. John 10:14-16 says: "I am the good shepherd; I know my sheep and my sheep know me. . . . They too will listen to my voice, and there shall be one flock and one shepherd."

If you wish to start a personal ministry, first be sure you have a relationship with the Lord. He speaks softly, and you won't be able to hear his direction unless you are close to him.

2. Pray continually. Romans 12:12 tells us to be "prayerful always," yet when we observe Christ's life in Scripture, we see he wasn't constantly on his knees. He had work to do, and he went about it daily. But Christ had an attitude of constant communion with his heavenly Father. He sought his Father's guidance in everything he did. So should we.

3. Ask for specific direction. If you have an idea for a personal ministry, take that idea to God and ask for his direction. Is it really his plan for you, or is it coming from some need for recognition? If you are still looking for a way you can give back, ask God. Ezekiel 36:37 tells us that "The Lord God says: I am ready to hear . . . and to grant them their requests. Let them but ask" (TLB).

Yvonne Martinez prayed for specific direction. As an adult child of divorce and a victim of rape, Yvonne spent several years in the healing process. When she was asked to share her story with some women, their lives were touched. Soon Yvonne's church approached her to head up a support group for victims. Many support groups later, Yvonne now spends much of her time teaching others how to lead support groups.

4. Wait for the Lord. Many of us today are accustomed to instant everything—fast food, speedy service. Waiting is not a welcome part of our life. Yet it is often part of God's plan for us. Psalm 27:14 says: "Don't be impatient. Wait for the Lord. . . . Yes, wait and he will help you" (TLB). When you have to wait, remember—it'll be worth it.

5. Weigh your answer. When we *think* we have an answer to our prayers, it's important to *confirm* that answer with Scripture. If the Bible doesn't directly address the issue, seek wise counsel.

6. Thank God. Once God has confirmed the direction of our own personal ministry, we must thank him. Philippians 4:6 sums it up perfectly: "Don't worry about anything; instead, pray about everything; tell God your needs, and don't forget to thank him for his answers" (TLB).

IN MY RELATIONSHIP WITH GOD, I'D LOVE TO BE POISED IN all situations, eager to hear whatever he's saying to me through his Holy Spirit, and ready to respond with obedience. But how? As responsibilities to friends, family, church, and work fight to claim our attention, simply having regular devotions can feel like a tremendous accomplishment. If that's how you feel, here are some tips by author Leigh Wilkins for distinguishing the voice of the Holy Spirit over the clamor of your world:

TUNE IN TO THE HOLY SPIRIT
LEIGH WILKINS

 ACTIVELY SEEK HIM Most of us don't know the Holy Spirit very well, even though without him, we'd be unable to live in a way that pleases God. In the days before Jesus' birth, the Holy Spirit only came upon certain prophets, priests, and kings for short periods of time to accomplish specific tasks. Before his crucifixion, Jesus explained that the Spirit would soon come upon all believers—which happened at Pentecost. In our day the Spirit lives in us from the moment we accept Christ as Savior, and our awareness of him grows as we mature in our relationship with God.

The Holy Spirit is one with God the Father and Jesus the Son, with distinct responsiblities in helping us live the Christian life. He fills many roles, empowering us to share the gospel (Acts 1:8), equipping us for service (1 Cor. 12:7-11), helping us to pray (Rom. 8:26), reminding us of who we are in Christ (1 John 4:13), and much more. If you'd like to learn more about the Holy Spirit, read through the eighth chapter of Romans or the entire book of Acts, where his power was evident in the early days of the church. You could also start a Bible study on the Holy Spirit, use a concordance to cross-reference the word *Spirit*

in your Bible, or see what Jesus had to say about the Spirit in the Gospel of John.

 RECOGNIZE HOW HE WORKS IN YOUR LIFE The more you get to know the Holy Spirit, the more you'll recognize him in your thoughts and day-to-day experiences.

How does the Holy Spirit work in your life? One way to find out is to pray that God will show you. Take note of how he answers those prayers! You may sense the Spirit's guidance through a "chance" encounter with just the right person, a gentle but persistent thought, or a Scripture verse that suddenly comes to mind.

 RESPOND GLADLY TO THE SPIRIT'S LEADING Being aware of how the Spirit works in my life doesn't mean much unless I obey him promptly. The challenge comes when obedience defies common sense, looks foolish, and isn't easy!

 TAKE GOD'S WORD SERIOUSLY There is an inextricable connection between God's Word and the Holy Spirit. In Ephesians 6:17, the apostle Paul notes that "the sword of the Spirit . . . is the word of God," meaning that the Spirit relies on the truth of God's Word to win our spiritual battles. So, in order to hear God clearly, we need to believe that what he says in the Bible is true. Any attempt to recognize the Holy Spirit without the wholehearted support of Scripture can produce disastrous results (such as a Christian who "missionary-dates" or marries a non-Christian because she doesn't feel God telling her to break it off).

 ENJOY THE REWARDS OF A SPIRIT-LED LIFE I'm thankful for a God who cares so much about his children that he sends the Holy Spirit to guide us, not just through the big decisions of life, but in the most ordinary, everyday circumstances as well. In doing so, God accomplishes an even greater purpose of drawing us closer to him. And that's something worth tuning in to!

DO YOU STRUGGLE WITH BEING UNGRATEFUL? WITH
viewing things that happen in a negative light? Maybe your work
is too intense or requires traveling or too many hours out of your
day. Maybe you wish you married a different person—or had a
husband. Perhaps you wish for a bigger apartment, a nicer house
or car, or better-behaved children.

When we're discouraged, it's easier to look at what we
don't have, rather than what we do. If that's how you feel right
now, here's how you can learn to be truly grateful:

Be Grateful

MADALENE HARRIS

As a young mom, I figured I had a lot to complain about.
For ten years my husband traveled continuously and left
me alone with four children to raise. It seemed as if every
week the babies became ill, the older children got into a
fight, the washing machine conked out, or the car broke
down! When things didn't go my way, I complained loud
and long. I justified my behavior because trying to juggle
the roles of mom, housekeeper, nurse, chauffeur, referee,
disciplinarian—and anything else that popped up—was far
from easy!

One day during that bleak period, my Bible study teacher
focused her lesson on two verses: "In all things God works for
the good of those who love him" (Rom. 8:28), and "Give
thanks in all circumstances (1 Thess. 5:18). As I listened, I
realized little genuine gratitude characterized *my* Christian
life—and I certainly didn't have the inner peace, faith, contentment, and positive attitude that a grateful heart generates.

Fortunately for my kids and my husband, I decided to
begin reversing my pattern of ungratefulness and moving
toward gratitude. Here's how:

1. Make a deliberate choice to give thanks. I began my journey toward gratitude by memorizing 1 Thessalonians 5:18: "Give thanks in all circumstances, for this is God's will for you in Christ Jesus." I determined to quote that verse many times each day so I could begin to see the positive side of life's events. I *chose* to be thankful instead of complaining.

2. Transfer your focus from circumstances to God. Just five years ago, my friend Kim—a vibrant, successful career woman—suffered damage to her central nervous system in an automobile accident that wasn't her fault. Kim will never be free of intense pain and progressive disability. But she made a conscious choice to transfer her focus from the hopelessness of her condition to God and his goodness. Instead of complaining, she's become a tireless intercessor—and a continual joy to be around.

3. Look on the bright side. Author Henri Nouwen, in *Life of the Beloved,* writes that we've all missed chances to be grateful. "When someone is kind to us, when an event turns out well, when a problem is solved, a relationship restored, a wound healed—these are concrete reasons to offer thanks."

4. Wait and see. God asks us to give thanks in *advance*—before we see or know the consequences. Thirteen years ago, even after several years of practicing gratitude, I was *not* grateful when a biopsy confirmed the presence of cancer in my husband, Harlan. We couldn't imagine how cancer could ever work for our good and God's glory. Back then, how could we guess that Harlan would experience years of remission—and that some of his finest ministry would occur during those years? No textbook ever contained the lessons we learned of faith, patience, endurance, and compassion.

Anyone can choose a grateful heart instead of a bitter one. Will you?

HOW DO YOU GROW WITH GOD? DO YOU SET ASIDE A regular time for prayer and Bible study? go to church weekly? get away for a retreat once a year? When Susannah Wesley, mother of hymn writers Charles and John Wesley, had little time alone because of her young and numerous brood, she began putting her apron over her head to signal to the children that she was praying and didn't wish to be disturbed. Now *that's* creativity!

There are many creative ways to grow with God. As you read the following tips from these well-known women, think up your own—and put one into action this week!

GROW WITH GOD

 PLAN A QUIET SPOT IN YOUR DAY I try to carve out at least thirty minutes each morning for prayer and Bible reading. My day starts better—and ends better—when I have my quiet time. I also meet once a week with a friend for Bible study.

ELIZABETH DOLE

 REFLECT CHRIST Worship isn't just what you do on Sunday or at a particular time during a church service. You worship God by the way you live your life, and that attracts others to God, too. When you reflect Christ in all aspects of your life, people who come in contact with you won't be able to deny that the message of the gospel is real and offers hope.

TWILA PARIS

 SURRENDER TO GOD When I realize how great God is, my problems become so small. There's no reason to worry anymore. No wonder the devil tries so hard to keep us too busy to pray!

There's so much God wants to do for us, but many times he doesn't work in our life because we're not ready for

him. God wants a relationship with us, but he patiently
waits for us to allow him fully into our life. Perhaps that's
why the hymn "I Surrender All" has become my
favorite—because that's something I constantly try to do:
Turn everything over to God.

CeCe Winans

 GET INVOLVED After attending a women's Bible study and
discipleship group weekly for many years, this year I took
the plunge and offered to lead a group myself. Whenever I
feel insecure, I remember God doesn't wait for us to
"arrive" before he can use us. He sees us not only as we
are now but as we will be.

Junko Cheng

 BE QUIET The more we allow ourselves to shut off the noise
of the world, be alone, and study the Bible, the less
important the things of this life become and the more we
want to please God, to live according to his standards.
Worshiping God isn't an emotional state—it's living in a
way that honors him, no matter what the cost.

Kay Arthur

 SEE GOD AND HIS CREATION AS AWESOME The quietest,
most lovely times I've ever had are sitting on the beach of
Lake Tahoe, looking out over the mountains and
water—God's marvelous creations. My soul just cries out,
Wow, God! You are awesome, and nothing else matters.
The Lord is much bigger than we think, much bigger than
we can imagine.

Bodie Thoene

 BE FAITHFUL The key is to look at what God puts in your
path today, then do it with all your might. Learn to be
faithful in the small tasks. Spirituality is bringing the
essence of Jesus Christ into the space that you
occupy—and you can do that wherever you are.

Carol Kent

WHEN YOU HEAR THE WORD *EVANGELISM*, WHAT RUNS through your mind? Maybe it's *I can't do that. I'm too shy.* Or *That's not my gifted area.* Or perhaps, *I'd love to tell others about Christ. But how?*

Sharing your faith is easier than it may first look. You don't need a Bible background or years of being a Christian. All you need is a caring heart, and a willingness for God to use you. So the next time the Holy Spirit nudges you, try these nonthreatening ways to share your faith—and watch them work!

Spread the Word

LIZ CURTIS HIGGS

In 1981, I was as far away from righteous living as a woman could get. Then a husband-and-wife team, who were new in Christ, started working at the radio station where I was the host of the midday show.

This couple didn't know tons of Bible verses yet, but they knew Jesus Christ. They hadn't memorized the Four Spiritual Laws, but they knew how to care about people. Simply put, they invited me into their home, welcomed me into their lives, and loved me into the family of God.

Months later I followed their example and shared my limited but enthusiastic knowledge of the Lord with two work friends—with the same surprising result. I wrote their names in the margin of my Bible, right next to 1 Thessalonians 2:8: "We loved you so much that we were delighted to share with you not only the gospel of God but our lives as well, because you had become so dear to us."

Many years and many changed lives later, I'm convinced sharing your faith simply requires caring enough about someone else to let that person know how Christ has changed your life. This simple method is the most effective way to, as my pastor says, "take as many people with us as possible" to heaven. Here are seven specific ways to prepare people's hearts for the Good News:

BE THERE FOR THEM

Romans 12:15 tells us to "rejoice with those who rejoice; mourn with those who mourn." Is someone having a birthday at work? Be the first to have a card waiting on her desk. Is a friend struggling with two toddlers? Stop by with a bucket of chicken at dinnertime. Such ministry is common in the church family but uncommon outside the church. Your attention to your coworkers' or neighbors' needs will really stand out!

Most of us believe that faith in Christ brings contentment, peace, and joy. So when we still experience fear, we feel like a spiritual failure! However, we can continue to respond with fearful emotions— or recognize God's power to help.

CAROL KENT

BE GENEROUS WITH YOUR RESOURCES

Proverbs 22:9 says, "A generous man will himself be blessed, for he shares his food with the poor." My friend Evelyn, who introduced me to the Lord, got my attention early in our friendship when she did exactly as this verse suggests. Ev and her husband, Tim, arrived at the radio station one morning and found a woman digging through the Dumpster looking for something to sell or eat. When their offer of money was abruptly refused, Ev came up with a better plan.

The next morning she arrived much earlier than usual and stuffed cans of food in the Dumpster. Not only did she demonstrate generous concern for the hungry woman, but my spiritually hungry soul was fed, too, when I heard about her good deed. I remember thinking, *So that's what it means to be a Christian!*

LOVE, DON'T JUDGE

I need to hear Matthew 7:1 so often, it's practically my life verse: "Do not judge, or you too will be judged." Early in my

Christian walk, I confronted a woman in my Bible study who was just beginning to explore the notion of Christianity. "If you're going to study God's Word, your boyfriend has to move out of your apartment!" I told her. She moved out of the Bible study instead—and it took weeks of repair work to restore our friendship.

Thank God for a happy ending—she accepted Christ—but I'm more careful now to love rather than judge. It's the Holy Spirit's business to convict, not ours.

BE AN ENCOURAGER

Hebrews 3:13 urges us to "encourage one another daily, as long as it is called Today." In other words, don't let the sun go down on your encouragement! Consider what you could do today to uplift someone who needs it.

CHOOSE YOUR WORDS CAREFULLY

Proverbs 25:11 declares, "A word aptly spoken is like apples of gold in settings of silver." I've also learned—the hard way—that the wrong word spoken in the wrong place at the wrong time is like rotten apples in a hot car. Ugh!

SAY YOU'LL PRAY—THEN DO IT

The apostle Paul wrote in Romans 1:9-10: "How constantly I remember you in my prayers at all times." On a late evening trip to Detroit, a flight attendant strolled the aisle of our nearly empty plane, glanced over my shoulder at the book I was reading, and asked, "What's that about?"

I grinned. It was Becky Pippert's classic book on lifestyle evangelism, *Out of the Salt Shaker and into the World*. "It's about how to share your faith."

Her eyebrows went up. "Really?" In a casual, matter-of-fact way, I briefly shared my journey from a party-hearty lifestyle of drugs and promiscuity to a new life of joy and purpose in Christ.

Sitting down across the aisle, she said, "It's made that

much of a difference for you, huh?" At that moment the pilot announced our approach to Detroit Metro Airport. As she jumped up to resume her duties, I glanced at her name tag.

"Christine, when I get to my hotel room tonight, I'd love to pray for you. Do you mind?"

Her eyes opened wide. "Would you really pray for me?"

"I'd be honored," I assured her, opening the back cover of my book and jotting her name down. Her teary thank-you before she headed up the aisle spoke volumes about the power of prayer, even to those who don't yet know the Lord.

> *God delights in using people who don't feel adequate. Why? Because then we know, beyond the shadow of a doubt, he's the one who did it—not us. And he gets the praise.*
>
> CECE WINANS

BE FEARLESSLY BOLD!

Sometimes you need to be gentle in your witness, but other moments call for bolder measures. In such situations, a Bible verse like 1 Peter 3:13 can be a great comfort: "Who is going to harm you if you are eager to do good?"

When I boldly said no to my station manager when he requested I feature an hour of call-ins with a psychic, he was shocked. "OK," he finally said with a disappointed sigh, "but I think you're missing a great opportunity to increase your ratings."

Boldly saying no in the cause of Christ produced fruit in the months that followed. The ratings went up (without the psychic), and the program director became a Christian and married a precious sister in Christ. I love happy endings!

Sharing the gospel isn't so much what you know as *whom* you know. If you know the Savior and are surrounded by friends and family who haven't met him yet, then who better to handle the introductions than you?

HAVE YOU EVER BEEN IN PAIN FOR A PERIOD OF TIME AND wondered if it would ever end? That's how I felt the summer I had knee surgery, hand surgery, *and* my wisdom teeth removed. But it was during that time of "nonmovement" that I began, at first out of boredom, to write out Scripture verses on index cards. That very fall those promises kept my faith strong and growing when one friend was killed in a car accident, another tried to commit suicide, and a third was diagnosed with cancer.

God's promises are powerful. They can change your life, others', and even a nation. That's what this next story is about.

Live by God's Promises

ELIZABETH MITTELSTAEDT

Ten years ago I spent five hours in a dentist's chair for a "routine" dental procedure and was left with a severely damaged nerve in my jaw. To rid myself of the excruciating pain, I traveled from one doctor to another for six months— to no avail. Finally, a doctor at the Mayo Clinic in Minnesota said, "There's nothing more we can do to repair the damage or relieve your pain. You'll have to live with it."

When I returned home to Germany with this news, I was deeply depressed. Death felt like the only escape. However, as a Christian, I knew it wasn't God's will to take my life, but rather, a temptation. Yet the constant pain took its toll. I felt hopeless. One day during my morning walk, I crossed a small bridge near Frankfurt, looked down at the flowing river below, and was tempted to jump. At that moment Matthew 4:5-7 came to mind. I recalled how the devil had unsuccessfully tempted Jesus to jump from the highest point of the temple. So I said, "No, I am *not* going to jump. I am going to trust God."

I began telling God what I was most afraid of—living in pain. Then I remembered that Jesus says we shouldn't worry about tomorrow—that he gives us strength for each day. I thought, *Somehow, I'll make it through this day*.

As I looked out over our town's fairy-tale homes with flower-filled window boxes, white picket fences, and clean-swept sidewalks, I realized that behind this perfect facade were thousands of women struggling with broken marriages, depression, guilt, and loneliness. I felt God speak to my heart, *These women are suffering like you, but their pain is different—it's emotional*.

I no longer felt so alone in my pain. Suddenly I was filled with a desire to encourage these women. That morning the vision for a Christian woman's magazine in Europe was born.

Almost a decade has passed since that day by the bridge. Today, *Lydia* is printed in three languages and reaches a million readers. Its message is simple—hope and encourage-ment can be found through faith in Christ and his Word. When I receive letters from readers who say, "I didn't abort my baby, and I'm naming her Lydia after the magazine," or "Thank you—this magazine is my friend," my heart is thrilled.

Pain is still my companion—but it's no longer as over-whelming as it once was. When I searched God's Word for encouragement and comfort, I came upon Psalm 34:19: "Many are the afflictions of the righteous: but the Lord delivereth him out of them all" (KJV). The words to the left of the colon describe my circumstances—and the words to the right give me real hope for the future. But I've learned that when we hang on to the colon in the middle—wait in faith on God's promise and offer our pain to him—it's never wasted.

THINK IT OVER
In what areas do you need to grow spiritually? Your prayer life? church attendance? trusting God? showing your gratitude? finding your ministry niche? sharing your faith with others? Ask God today to give you his wisdom and insight—and then pay attention to the Spirit's nudgings in your life.

Work

Life is more than a few years spent on
self-indulgence or career advancement.
It's a privilege, a responsibility, a stewardship
to be met according to God's calling.

ELIZABETH DOLE

IS YOUR WORK MEANINGFUL—
AND BALANCED?

HOW much of your day do you spend working? If you're a "9 to 5er," eight hours. If you're a student, four hours of studying for each class hour. If you're a new mom, twenty-four hours a day!

Whether you work part-time, full-time, in or outside the home, work is an important part of your day. The start of "work" is recorded in the book of Genesis: "By the seventh day God had finished the work he had been doing; so on the seventh day he rested from all his work" (2:2). And because God is a purposeful creator, he also gave us jobs to do: "The Lord God took the man and put him in the Garden of Eden to work it and take care of it" (2:15).

Yes, work should be meaningful, but nowhere in the Bible does God say that work should overtake our life. In this busy world, how can we keep our balance? That's what this chapter is about.

IF SOMEONE ASKED YOU WHO YOU ARE, WHAT WOULD you say? Would you define yourself as a professional? wife? mom? Psychologists say that while men traditionally define themselves through their careers, women typically have defined themselves by their relationships. Yet as more women enter the workplace, they, too, are basing their identities on their work.

If you wonder sometimes who you really are, outside of all your roles, meet Janis Long Harris—and other women—who've also experienced an identity crisis and have lived to tell about it.

Remember: Work Doesn't Make You Who You Are

JANIS LONG HARRIS

Melicent Huneycutt knows firsthand the emotional devastation that results from the loss of a familiar role. When she suddenly found herself jobless as a single woman in her late fifties, the former missionary and college professor felt like a "nonperson."

"I felt it the most when I went to parties and realized I had no way to introduce myself," she says. "Since I wasn't anybody's wife or mother and I didn't have a job, the only way I could identify myself was to tell people my name. It was a very difficult period."

I went through a similarly difficult time shortly after my daughter was born. Wanting to spend as much time with her as possible, I decided to work at home rather than immediately return to the workplace. I quickly discovered I'd underestimated how much having a title, office, and regular paycheck contributed to my sense of self. I was thrilled to be a mother—but I mourned the loss of my identity as a briefcase-carrying career woman.

Some women I know have gone through the opposite experience. My friend Barbara, for example, spent most of her adult life happily raising four children. But when her youngest son went off to college, Barbara found herself adrift. "I felt I had no purpose in life anymore," she recalls.

She briefly took a job as a receptionist at a bank but found her new role as a working woman an unsatisfying substitute for the one she missed so desperately.

Whatever we do, we need to do it with excellence.

KAY COLES JAMES

Melicent, Barbara, and I made the same mistake—we based our identities on external life circumstances that are subject to change. But recognizing the problem is easier than finding a solution. How can women like us—who nonetheless live in a rough-and-tumble world of changing roles and relationships—discover our true identities?

Here are some guidelines I've gleaned from firsthand experience—as well as from other women who've struggled with identity issues and won:

MAKE YOUR RELATIONSHIP TO GOD THE FOUNDATION OF YOUR IDENTITY

The first step in developing a true identity is to establish a strong *spiritual* identity rooted in a relationship with God— the only truly reliable relationship that exists.

When Melicent started to ask herself, Who am I really? for the first time in almost sixty years, she knew where to go. Scripture, the source of her knowledge about God, suddenly became the source of knowledge about herself.

"I was struck with the first chapter of Ephesians," Melicent recalls. "It describes how those in Christ were chosen before the foundation of the earth. I began to envision how God knew me from the very beginning—how he planned my red hair, green eyes, and fair skin. I realized that if God valued me for who I was that much, I should value myself as well."

DISCOVER YOUR SPIRITUAL GIFTS

Finding your true identity almost always requires a knowledge of your spiritual gifts.

"Our identities often have more to do with our attributes, values, and gifts than with our actions," says psychologist Beverly Grall. "Our gifts comprise the core of our being—they define who we are totally apart from how we choose to use them in life."

For example, a woman who defines herself as a mother may be devastated when her children grow up. But a woman who defines herself as someone with a talent for nurturing will retain her identity and find other ways to express it—even when confronted with an empty nest.

That's what happened with my friend Barbara. She discovered her ability to care for and help others—a gift she used so well in parenting—was needed by many social service organizations. Today she serves as a volunteer for several organizations and knows her identity can withstand any changing circumstances.

But how do you go about discovering your gifts? One woman I know offers this suggestion: "Start paying attention to yourself and what you really like. Ask yourself, What do I really enjoy doing? What makes me feel productive? I've found that when I'm really walking the way God foreordained me to walk, I feel refreshed. When some activity drains me, it may be because I'm fulfilling a role assigned to me by someone else's expectations."

Here are some other suggestions for discovering your gifts: Think back on those areas in life in which you've received affirmation. If others consistently tell you you are gifted in a particular area, they may be right. Also, try to identify activities and experiences that have held your attention in such a way that you stopped thinking about yourself and concentrated solely on the task. If you can find such activities, they may be in the area of your giftedness.

When I considered these principles, I realized I could exercise my most obvious gifts—my ability to listen well, articulate, and analyze—whether or not I was in an office.

As I worked on deriving my identity more from the gifts I had than from a specific way to exercise them, I gradually stopped mourning the loss of my self-definition as a career woman.

USE PAINFUL EVENTS AS A SOURCE OF GROWTH

Questioning who we are is never easy, but it can serve a useful role—if you let it.

"Pain gets our attention," says psychologist Grall. "We often grow much closer to God when we've experienced brokenness. In the same way, we often become better acquainted with *ourselves* when we go through difficult experiences as well."

Perhaps because I've lost a husband and children, eternity has become more real to me. I know this life is going to speed by, and I want to pour all I've got into doing something for God's kingdom.

MELODY GREEN

I can attest to that. I probably never would have been sufficiently motivated to seriously inventory my gifts—and consequently develop who I am in Christ as my foundation—had I not experienced the pain and emptiness of losing my identity.

The process wasn't particularly enjoyable. Emptying yourself of an old identity can be scary, uncertain, and exhausting. But it's important.

Why?

Because God needs space in which to do his work. As a result of his work—and some of my own—I now feel much more confident in who I am in Christ, in whatever circumstances or work I find myself. And that's a liberating feeling.

GETTING TO WORK. GETTING THROUGH WORK. GETTING home from work. If even reading these words raises your stress level or gets you "down in the dumps," you're not the only one. Our workdays alone are enough—meetings, deadlines, relating (or not) to coworkers and supervisors—to make us cry "Uncle!" And that doesn't even include the personal things we juggle during our workday—lunch with a friend, breastfeeding during breaks, grocery shopping to fill an almost empty refrigerator. Being a working woman *is* stressful, no doubt about it. But these tips from working-woman expert Mary Whelchel will help you not feel overwhelmed:

Find Ways to Reduce Workplace Stress

MARY WHELCHEL

Stress affects all areas of our life. Quite frankly, I think the woman in the workplace often deals with excessive amounts of stress because of her many responsibilities and heavy workload.

I've discovered some extremely practical stress reducers based on biblical principles that you can incorporate into your daily lifestyle. I practice these regularly because I tend to be a high-stress person.

1. Slow down and be still. Often I rush when there is no reason to. Our society is build on speed, and that causes us a great deal of stress. David wrote, "Be still before the Lord and wait patiently for him" (Ps. 37:7). Yet in our world, it's not so simple to slow down. We have to work at it.

Remind yourself daily to slow down. Commit a short, motivating verse to memory like "Be still, and know that I am God" (Ps. 46:10), and repeat it to yourself each time you feel tension building.

2. Get together with an upbeat friend or coworker who has a good sense of humor and laugh. In Proverbs we read that a cheerful heart is good medicine. Just notice the people around you; the cheerful ones who laugh a lot usually aren't as tense or stressed out as the ones who don't.

3. Take a moment to relive a happy time in your life or a successful day in the office. Scripture reminds us that we should remember all the good things God has done for us. Asaph wrote in Psalm 77:11, "I will remember the deeds of the Lord; yes, I will remember your miracles of long ago." So remember how God delivered you in the past. Recite out loud those occasions of joy and thanksgiving. You'll be amazed at how that lifts your spirits and reduces stress.

4. Try talking less and listening more. If you're a talker like me, you can reduce your stress by reducing the number of words you say. If your mouth isn't always in motion, you'll be more likely to listen. Learning to really listen to others and then choosing your words with restraint can reduce your stress. You'll be thinking more clearly and making better decisions. Often the more words we say, the more confusing something becomes.

5. Live in the present. Jesus told us not to borrow trouble from yesterday or tomorrow. Don't worry about the big meeting you have the next day, and don't continually review the mistakes you made at work yesterday. Many of us need to practice this because a great deal of our stress is due to our tendency to worry about the past or fear what's going to happen in the future. As simple as it sounds, learn to live one day at a time.

TWO YEARS AGO, WHEN HER HUSBAND TOOK A DIP IN salary due to a company takeover, my friend Sarah, a mom of two, began typing a few hours a week for a local company. When I asked how she managed all her tasks, her reply was simple: "I keep my home life and my work separate." When she had a typing deadline, she closed the door on her laundry. When her husband and kids arrived home, she put away her work.

If you work at home and struggle with "getting it all done," try these simple tips:

SEPARATE YOUR HOME AND WORK LIFE IF YOU WORK AT HOME

💡 RESERVATIONS, PLEASE If you have young children, set aside certain periods of the day or week that are reserved for your work. Nap times are always good, but you may need more work time than that.
MARY WHELCHEL

💡 WORKING 9 TO 5 Develop a work/projects calendar and keep office hours at home. When the "five o'clock whistle" blows, turn off the lights and close your office door.
ELAINE K. MCEWAN-ADKINS

💡 HIRE SOME HELP Instead of being obsessive about cleaning my house and having to stay up late to do it, I hired someone to clean every other week. I was amazed to find out it was affordable!
CAROL KENT

💡 FAMILY FORUM Talk about your workload with family members. Explain your responsibilities and deadlines so they'll understand your need for privacy or silence.
ELAINE K. MCEWAN-ADKINS

💡 SAY NO TO OVERCOMMITMENT I have a calendar-marking system—a circled day means a ministry day, and an under-lined day is saved for my family. No matter who calls, that day is already taken. If I don't make choices based on my priorities, my whole life would be planned for me.

CAROL KENT

 CAUTION! Learn to be realistic and say no. Don't fall into the trap of volunteering to do everything "just because you're not working full-time." People who know you work at home don't realize you have to be twice as organized and work twice as hard to be successful in a home-based business.

ELAINE K. MCEWAN-ADKINS

 HANDY HELPER If you have young children, ask a neighborhood girl or relative to watch the kids for you in the afternoons while you work. It wouldn't cost a great deal, and the kids would probably enjoy having someone new to play with. You could teach them that they are not to disturb you when the sitter is there.

MARY WHELCHEL

 FAMILY FIRST Don't allow your work to interfere with your family life. Don't schedule appointments with clients when your children are due to arrive home from school or are on school holidays and need your attention.

ELAINE K. MCEWAN-DKINS

 DON'T TRY TO BE "SUPERWOMAN" A little dust on the furniture isn't going to cause serious problems! Simplify your life and duties as much as possible.

MARY WHELCHEL

 TAKE A DAY OFF Take a day off occasionally to do those things you promised yourself you would do when you had more freedom.

ELAINE K. MCEWAN-ADKINS

 KEEP YOUR PRIORITIES STRAIGHT I've learned that if I keep my priorities straight—God first, family second, ministry and career last—God will work everything else out.

CECE WINANS

HOME. HUSBAND. CAREER. CHILDREN. CHURCH.
Relationships. These are just a few of the responsibilities that we, as women, juggle every day. Though wonderful, they add up to a lot of work! If you're continually feeling overwhelmed with your life responsibilities, maybe it's time to do some self-evaluation. Following are some key questions to ask yourself. And, in the process, remember that life has its seasons and that some times will be busier than others—and that's OK!

Downscale If You're Overwhelmed

MARY WHELCHEL

During the last three decades, women have been led to believe they can have it all. But now a major change in women's attitudes toward the workplace is occurring. Many women are beginning to evaluate their work, asking themselves, Is the rat race worth it? Are my workplace accomplishments bringing satisfaction? How is my higher stress affecting my family?

If you are in the process of deciding what is worthwhile and what isn't, consider the following checkpoints before you make your decision:

- Am I tired and exhausted a lot of the time, with little or no energy left for my family, friends, or church?
- What motivates me to keep climbing the career ladder?
- Who am I trying to impress with my accomplishments?
- How am I using the success I have gained? Is it a vehicle to share Christ with the world, or is it solely for personal gain?
- How much has my standard of living risen in the last five years? Do I now consider luxuries necessities?

■ How much of my week in hours is devoted to my career?
Is it reasonable?

These questions will help you assess your attitude toward your career—whether it is controlling you or you are controlling it. If you feel that too much of your life is consumed with your job, consider downscaling. That may mean working part-time, finding a less demanding position, or quitting work altogether—if that is an option.

More and more companies are allowing employees to work part-time or out of their homes. You might want to submit a proposal for part-time work that is advantageous for your company, such as a reduction in your benefits package. Make them an offer. Just because they've not done it before doesn't mean they won't do it.

When a successful lawyer I know had a child, she worked out a deal with her firm to work three days a week. Another friend worked out an arrangement with her employer, a publisher, to edit books from her home when her son was born. She sets aside a few hours each day while her son is sleeping, and it's working out beautifully.

Downscaling usually requires a willingness to lower your standard of living. The vacations may become simpler, the dinners out will decrease, the wardrobe probably will shrink. But these are small sacrifices to bring your life into balance.

When I began my radio ministry seven years ago, I downscaled from a full-time management position to part-time self-employment as a business trainer.

There's no question I could triple my income if I poured all my time and energy into my business. But I made a decision to downscale—earn enough money to pay my bills—and use the remainder of my time for a unique ministry to workplace women. My choice has not been a sacrifice; each year my satisfaction has gone up!

DO YOU EVER WISH YOU HAD JUST ONE DAY WITH
nothing to do except what *you* wanted to do, with no strings
attached? Or even that your day weren't quite so full of activities
or people? The older I get, the more I realize how important
balance is in life—a little play, some work, and all in the context
of enhancing old relationships and growing new ones. I know in
theory that balance is a good thing, but accomplishing it is
another story. If you, like me, struggle with life balance, here are
some handy tips.

STRIVE FOR BALANCE IN EVERYTHING YOU DO

 DON'T OVERWORK If you find yourself overworking,
  analyze why you spend so much time on your job. Too
  much of anything—even work you love—can lead to
  burnout. If you're working to gain approval from others or
  prove something to someone, then you're expecting your
  job to fulfill you, and that is a mistake. As Christians, we
  must find our joy and meaning in Jesus alone. Make
  certain your love for Jesus is the focus of your existence.
  MARY WHELCHEL

RELAX YOUR STANDARDS Piles of laundry, dishes, bills—it's
  tough to see such things lying around the house because
  we feel the mess reflects who we are. During such times,
  it's important to remember that relationships are more
  important than things. So the next time you're running
  around frazzled, trying to vacuum before your guests
  arrive, stop. Take a deep breath—and a few minutes'
  break. Your guests are coming to see *you*, not your house.
  RAMONA CRAMER TUCKER

AVOID LAST-MINUTE-ITIS Try to avoid last-minute crunches, like agreeing to meet impossible deadlines either at home or work.

ELAINE K. MCEWAN-ADKINS

 AWAY WITH PERFECTIONISM! I used to think that if something wasn't done perfectly, it shouldn't be done. But finally I acknowledged it was impossible for me to entertain the way my mother had—since I was in a traveling ministry, I couldn't always polish the silver and iron the linens. If I wanted to have people over, it was OK to bring pizza home, make a quick salad, and serve it on everyday dishes.

CAROL KENT

 REALIZE YOU'RE NOT STUCK Ask yourself, "If there were no limitations on you, what would you want to do? What is your passion—what keeps popping back into your mind?" Then ask God, "What are the plans you have for me?" Write out Psalm 37:4: "Delight yourself in the Lord and he will give you the desires of your heart."

So often we don't give God credit for letting us do what we really want to do. It's as though we think we're supposed to be miserable doing God's will. But when we fulfill God's plan, whether it's changing a diaper, teaching a class, or closing a deal, it becomes a delight.

KATHY PEEL

 LEARN TO DELEGATE If you're feeling overwhelmed, remember that others can help you—and that asking them doesn't mean you're incompetent in life.

RAMONA CRAMER TUCKER

 FOCUS ON GOD Sometimes it's hard to accept ourselves as we are, even when we burn dinner or forget an appointment. But when we focus on God and let him show us what he wants us to do, rather than let others set our life agenda, we are free to experience his joy.

JUNKO CHENG

DO YOU ENJOY YOUR WORK—OR IS IT A DAILY STRUGGLE? Do you feel unfulfilled? used? like a failure because you think you're not making a big enough contribution? Do you keep interviewing for jobs, only to be turned down repeatedly? If you're in any of these situations, you may have the work doldrums. Surprise—those feelings are natural! Why? Because God created us in his image as purposeful creatures, all of us crave meaningful work. So if your work is nonexistent or seems purposeless and exhausting right now, don't give up. You *can* rise above such setbacks. Here's how:

Rise above Setbacks

HOLLY G. MILLER

My friend Suzye, a social worker, recently told me the story of her first job—the dream position she had gone back to college at age thirty-five to achieve—and how she lost it ninety days later. Before she could settle into her new duties as a hospital social worker, the hospital announced a layoff, and Suzye received a pink slip.

Although the supervisor insisted the job loss had nothing to do with her skills and everything to do with the economy, Suzye saw it differently. "I was devastated," she says simply. "I felt as though I had failed at the job." She was convinced that if the hospital had *really* wanted her services, somehow she would have survived the cut. Burdened with feelings of rejection, she couldn't muster the confidence to look for another job.

"Then, out of the blue, the director of a nursing home called and invited me for an interview," Suzye recalls. "I never would have chosen that as an option, but after I visited the home and talked with the residents, I accepted the job offer."

She stayed almost seven years. "Looking back, I have no

doubt God wanted me there. Because of the people I met, I will never be the same. I learned what love is all about from couples who had been married sixty years."

Suzye's professional detour—she's once again working at a hospital— expanded her skills, added to her sensitivity, and reinforced her understanding of God's timing.

The greatest success we can have in life is to use the talents God has given us to fulfill his purposes.

DEBBYE TURNER

Despite our perceived or even very real setbacks, we can learn how to rise above failure and see God at work, too. Here's how:

LOOK FOR THE LESSON

What we lose—self-esteem, a relationship, status, job, money—usually is less important than how we react to that loss. Counselors who help people cope with defeats say our first response to "failure" should be to dissect it, not discard it. This advice holds true whether the failure involves a job, a marriage, or a New Year's resolution to lose ten pounds.

Every failure deserves a second look. Before turning our back on a setback, we need to search for hidden messages. Is God trying to tell us something?

SIZE UP THE FAILURE

Psychologists call it "awfulizing"—the tendency to inflate a small or midsize failure to catastrophic proportions. Those of us who have mastered the art of awfulizing can take a minor embarrassment and, within minutes, convince ourselves that the whole world is giggling at our expense.

Not long ago, when a friend handed me a card announcing her newly formed business as "bridal consultant," I asked, "But what if you fail?" envisioning financial disaster, ridicule, and a crushed ego. First, she looked surprised. Then she set me straight.

"My business might fail—but that doesn't make me a failure," she said.

My friend was right. I had equated her work with her worth and had imagined a potential failure in one area of her life spilling over to spoil every other area. My friend's words gently reminded me that we can be "hard pressed on every side, but not crushed" (2 Cor. 4:8) when we view ourselves from God's perspective.

SEND IT BACK TO WHERE IT BELONGS

Women, more than men, assume responsibility for failures they didn't cause and couldn't prevent. Because of our traditional roles as caretakers and nurturers, we feel a natural obligation to ensure that everyone is happy, comfortable, well fed, and properly entertained. Otherwise, it's our fault. But the key word is *control*. If a situation is beyond our control, we should take neither credit nor blame for it.

SHARE IT

"By sharing a failure, we realize we're not the first one to have made a mistake," says Rosalie, leader of a twelve-step group that reaches out to women in abusive situations. "We talk about it and pray about it. We collect affirmations that say we're OK, that the group likes us regardless of what's going on in our life."

Similar results occur when we talk privately with God. The burden becomes lighter, and the failure seems more manageable after we "pour out [our] hearts to him" (Ps. 62:8).

FORGIVE EVERYONE INVOLVED

In her work as a nursing-home social worker, Suzye frequently counseled elderly women still bitter about marriages that had failed thirty years earlier. Suzye's advice: Face the failure long enough to learn from it, exchange anger for insight, then move on. One of the most important insights is to recognize the need to forgive. If failure involves a loss, we must determine all the persons who had a hand in the loss—including ourselves—and forgive them. If the mistake was ours, we must ask God's forgiveness, then "forgive as the Lord forgave you" (Col. 3:13). Only then can we let go of the failure and move on.

In order for God to use you, you don't have to be part of an organized ministry or be specially talented. God can use you in whatever situation you are in today.

MARITA LITTAUER

RESET YOUR GOALS

Sometimes we set ourselves up for failure by creating impossible expectations we can never meet.

For years I was an incurable list maker, beginning each weekend by composing a long list of tasks I was determined to accomplish. Seldom working my way through half the entries, I faced the new week feeling tired and disappointed in myself. I might still be fighting my Sunday-night depression if friend and fellow list maker Helen Hosier hadn't helped me. "At the beginning of each week, I like to sit at my desk and strategize," Helen shared. "I say to myself, *This is a new week. What are you going to do with it?*" Then she closes her eyes and waits for God to provide the answer. And *that* makes all the difference.

RISK—IT'S WORTH IT!

Fear of failure can cause us to ignore God's gifts. However, as author and recording artist Gloria Gaither says, "The temptation is to stay with the status quo and not do anything to rock the boat. But if we succumb to that temptation, we might as well give up. I hope I'll always have the courage to take risks."

Every risk deserves much thought and prayer. But at some point, we have to trust God with the outcome and have faith that he will be with us in our defeats as well as our victories. Setbacks aren't always what they appear to be.

AH, HOUSEWORK. DUST BUNNIES IN CORNERS AND UNDER the couch, laundry that multiplies like rabbits, windows that always need washing. Housework is one job that never seems to end. As humorist Lucille Wilson quipped, "Housework is something you do that nobody notices unless you don't do it!" Following is hope and help for the housework weary. Mmmm . . . I think I need to read it again myself.

Keep Housework in Perspective

ELIZABETH CODY NEWENHUYSE

When my husband and I presented our certified check and signed twenty-seven different documents at the closing on our house, and in turn received house keys, deed, and sundry other papers, we proudly joined the ranks of the propertied classes. No more living under the guy who cranked up the bass speaker on his stereo at three in the morning. No more faceless white walls or landlords who seemed not to understand that toddlers draw on them. Finally, we'd be able to relax inside our very own walls.

Such innocents.

Now, five years later, we've learned—the hard way—that a house doesn't vacuum itself, mow its own grass, line its own kitchen cabinets, or clean its own closets. Houses are a never-ending drain of time and energy.

We've all heard the advice, "Let the cleaning go" and the verse, "Housework, be quiet; dust, go to sleep; I'm rocking my baby; and babies don't keep." We've all been told that, as we juggle jobs and families, we need to lower our housekeeping standards.

True, babies *don't* keep; my baby has turned into a freckled schoolkid seemingly overnight. At the same time, I think most of us desire to create a safe, clean, pleasant environment for our family. But why does it have to involve "toil-some labor"?

Everywhere I look I see *work*. There are days when house-hold "management" feels as futile as crawling on one's hands and knees around the Olympic track at Barcelona, rolling a marble with one's nose.

And it's not just the routine stuff. Sometimes you feel futile *before* you launch a major house project. You know it won't stay that way, and you don't have the energy to even try. For example, my spring cleaning has now turned into my fall cleaning, and I'll tell you why. Last May I had noble intentions: drapes to the dry cleaner; bedding aired; junk out of the basement; walls washed; closets straightened. I'd disinfect my kitchen cupboards and reline them with shelf paper. *This* would be the fresh start that would air out my very soul, the way spring's balmy breezes air out the winter-stuffy rooms of the house.

Somehow, the balmy breezes turned into the hot gusts of summer. Who cleans in summer? Before I knew it, my daughter was lobbying for a new school backpack, Ernie the giant sheepdog was growing his winter coat, and the toma-toes I forgot to cover had been killed by frost. And my yellowing to-do list remains affixed to my refrigerator.

Occasionally I wonder what it would be like to rent an apartment again. As I dust and scrub and declutter, world without end, I muse: Is there an enthusiastic, energetic young person somewhere who's just longing for the character-building experience of helping a nice Christian woman maintain her home?

Until I find her, I'll continue to push the marble around the track with my nose—or push the mop around the kitchen floor. And as my family sits around our kitchen table, enjoy-ing the meal and each other, I realize, *These people are the reason I do this*. They're a lot more important than my to-do list—which I just transferred to a sheet of legal-size paper.

THINK IT OVER

If someone asked you today, "How do you feel about your work?" what would you say? Maybe you're enthusiastic, loving what you do—good for you! Then again, maybe you're feeling continually unfulfilled or overwhelmed. If so, now's the time to begin thinking through your options (with your spouse, if you're married). If this is just a busy "season of life," these words may help: "If God calls you to do something, he'll equip you to do it."